A Grammar Manual

FOR CANADIAN E.S.L. STUDENTS

Volume A

Véra Téophil Naber

George Brown College of Applied Arts and Technology

Savitsa Sévigny

York University

PRENTICE HALL CANADA INC.

SCARBOROUGH, ONTARIO

Canadian Cataloguing in Publication Data

Naber, Véra Téophil
A grammar manual for Canadian ESL students
Volume A

ISBN 0-13-015330-3

1. English language – Textbooks for second language learners.*
2. English language – Grammar – 1950-
3. English language – Grammar – 1950-   - Problems,
exercises, etc. I. Sévigny, Savitsa. II. Title

PE1128.N33   1993   428.2'4   C92-095504-5

Prentice-Hall, Inc., Englewood Cliffs, New Jersey
Prentice-Hall International, Inc., London
Prentice-Hall of Australia, Pty., Ltd., Sydney
Prentice-Hall of India Pvt., Ltd., New Delhi
Prentice-Hall of Japan, Inc., Tokyo
Prentice-Hall of Southeast Asia (Pte.) Ltd., Singapore
Editora Prentice-Hall do Brasil Ltda., Rio de Janeiro
Prentice-Hall Hispanoamericana, S.A., Mexico

ISBN: 0-13-015330-3
Acquisitions Editor: Marjorie Munroe
Developmental Editor: Maryrose O'Neill
Copy Editor: Rebecca Vogan
Production Editors: Valerie Adams and Elise Levine
Page Layout and Design: Derek Chung
Illustration: Don Gauthier

1 2 3 4 5   BG   97 96 95 94 93

In memory of Natalie Percuklijeirc

Table of Contents

Preface
Acknowledgements

Preface

Description of the Text

A Grammar Manual for Canadian E.S.L. Students is a reference grammar for students of English as a second language, at a low intermediate level or for those students wishing to systematically review basic English structures. Though written for adults, it is also suitable for high school students whose native language is other than English.

A Grammar Manual for Canadian E.S.L. Students would also be a particular help to E.S.L. teachers as it provides them with a pedagogical tool for the introduction and teaching of grammatical structures.

Because it deals with common difficulties which E.S.L. students generally encounter, this manual can be used with equal success with native speakers of Chinese, Arabic, French, etc. Although we do not deny the value of contrastive analysis in second language pedagogy, it has been dealt with implicitly rather than explicitly.

Each unit comprises:

1. A grammar section with short explanations and charts to facilitate learning and retention. Each grammar section centres on a discrete point of grammar and is broken down into smaller sub-sections, each of which in turn takes up a certain aspect of the subject under study. These short sections constitute minimal steps which allow the students to understand and retain the material with relative ease. This also allows the teacher the flexibility to assign or cover any given section at a particular time.

2. A practice section which provides exercises asking the student to go from controlled responses to more open communicative activities. The sequence of exercises is designed to foster students' confidence as well students' oral and writing skills. The exercises themselves are varied and represent life-like situations. Usefulness to students and clarity of presentation were prime factors in our mode of presentation. Standard Canadian English is used throughout the text in the grammar, explanations, examples, and exercises. Colloquial expressions have been omitted.
    As this is not a beginner's text, pronunciation has not been dealt with systematically. It is only indicated when the written form could lead to pronunciation errors at this level.

Special Features

1. The units are sequenced to meet the evolving needs of intermediate students. For instance, although it is common practice to introduce the present continuous tense

early, we find that there are too many variations involved. Instead, this text introduces the simple tense early because it is easier to master and allows greater flexibility for expression. The present continuous can be (and is) dealt with more efficiently later in the course, when the student has gained greater knowledge and confidence.

2. The sequencing of the units is cumulative. If the order of presentation is followed, there will ensue systematic reinforcement of structures and materials in later units, thus enhancing the student's sense of mastery and achievement.

3. The units are self-contained. This modularity allows the instructor to alter the order followed in text to meet the special needs of students whose background may require an alternate sequencing and coverage.

4. In keeping with modern linguistic research findings concerning successful learning language, the simplest possible use of English has been used throughout to maximize motivation and a sense of achievement.

5. Vocabulary has been carefully chosen to avoid having the student tackle too many difficulties at once. For instance, in the first unit, international words such as tennis, piano, and music are used.

6. The manual can complement either the structural approach or the communicative approach.

Suggestions For the Use of the Manual

It is difficult to generalize about the timing needed as the linguistic needs may vary from one group to another. In general, the manual could constitute the grammar component of a course, equivalent to one of the following:

i)   a six-month course (with some of the material omitted)
ii) an intensive summer course
iii) a regular one-year full-time course (omitting little, if any, material)

The teacher could present the topics for study in class first or assign them as reading material in preparation for class discussion. Either should work equally well. In the matter of presentation of class discussion, the proceeding could go from rule to sentence production or sentence production to rule. Any approach is effective as long as the teacher takes into consideration the students' learning skills and modifies his/her teaching accordingly.

Acknowledgements

Special thanks to reviewers Jas Gill, English Language Institute, University of British Columbia, and Karen Hammond, Alberta Vocational College.

We wish to thank Ms. Marjorie Munroe, Ms. Valerie Adams and Ms. Maryrose O'Neill without whose assistance this manual could not have been published.

Our warmest thanks also go to Ms. Rebecca Vogan whose hard work and commitment have contributed a great deal both to the text and to the accompanying exercises.

We would like to also extend our thanks to Ms. Maureen Henriques, Ms. Elaine Blake and Ms. Elizabeth Kuzmas who typed our manuscript, as well as to Mr. Don Gauthier who looked after the artistic side of the book.

We are also indebted to numerous students at George Brown College who used this grammar while it was being tested in the classroom. Their comments and suggestions have led to considerable improvements in the text.

UNIT 1 – THE SIMPLE PRESENT TENSE AND THE IMPERATIVE

1.1   THE AFFIRMATIVE FORM

The simple present tense is formed with the **infinitive** – the base form of the verb, which is found in the dictionary – except in the third person singular.

I You We (Jim and I) They	SPEAK	English.

The letter *s* is added to the infinitive in the third person singular:

Mary (She) Antoine (He) The machine (It)	SPEAKS WORKS	English. very well.

Exception: In the third person singular, *have* changes to *has*.

I We She Ali	HAVE HAVE HAS HAS	a dictionary. a dictionary. a dictionary. a dictionary.

CHANGES IN SPELLING

a)   If the verb ends in *y*, change *y* to *ies*.

STUDY	STUDIES	Lam studies English.
TRY	TRIES	He tries hard.
		But: Savitsa **plays** the guitar.

b)   If the verb ends in *ch*, *sh*, *ss*, *x* or *o*, add *es*.

WATCH	WATCHES	Joe watches T.V. every night.
WASH	WASHES	He washes his hair every night.
MISS	MISSES	She misses her boyfriend.
FIX	FIXES	Bob fixes T.V. sets.
GO	GOES	Fatima goes shopping.

Note: The verb *be* changes in all persons. See Unit 4.

1.2   THE NEGATIVE FORM

The negative of the simple present tense is formed with ***do not*** (***don't*** in conversation) + Infinitive for all persons except the third person singular.

I		
You	DO NOT	
We (Tony and I)	or	SPEAK English.
They (Sam and Ly)	DON'T	

The third person singular is formed with **does not** (**doesn't** in conversation) + Infinitive.

Mary (She)		
	DOES NOT	SPEAK English.
Antoine (He)	or	
	DOESN'T	
The machine (It)		work very well.

1.3   THE INTERROGATIVE FORM

The interrogative of the simple present tense is formed with **does** for the third person and **do** for all other persons. *Does* and *do* come before the subject and the verb.

DO	I	SPEAK English?
	you	
	we (Jim and I)	
	they (Jim and Antoine)	
DOES	Mary (she)	SPEAK English?
	Antoine (he)	
	the machine	WORK very well?

1.4 *WHO*, *WHEN* AND *WHAT* QUESTIONS

An English sentence has a subject and a verb.
Lucy drives. (Subject: Lucy. *Verb:* drives.)
Sometimes the sentence has an object.
Lucy drives a truck. (Object: truck.)

WHO QUESTIONS

Who questions ask about persons. When *who* asks about the subject of the verb, we use the third person singular of the verb.

	Question	Response
WHO	wants a coke?	Jim. (Jim wants a coke.)
WHO	speaks French?	Nassir and Nader. (Nassir and Nader speak French.)
WHO	loves pizza?	I do. (I love pizza.)

When *who* asks about the object of the verb, we use the interrogative form of the verb.

	Question	Response
WHO	does Pam teach?	Chinese students. (She teaches Chinese students.)
WHO	do you work with?	Madeleine. (I work with Madeleine.)

WHEN QUESTIONS

When asks about the time.

	Question	Response
WHEN	do you play tennis?	On Sundays. (I play tennis on Sundays.)
WHEN	do the children want lunch?	Later. (They want lunch later.)
WHEN	does Rita study English?	Every day. (She studies English every day.)

WHAT QUESTIONS

What generally asks about things, animals, ideas and statements. It is used with or without the noun.

- Asking about **subjects**:
  What fruits grow in Ecuador?
  Bananas and mangoes. (Bananas and mangoes grow in Ecuador.)
  What grows in Italy?
  Grapes, figs and oranges. (Grapes, figs and oranges grow in Italy.)

- Asking about **objects**:
  What fruits do you grow in your garden?
  Peaches and pears. (I grow peaches and pears.)
  What does your neighbour grow?
  Cherries and apples. (She grows cherries and apples.)

- Asking a **general question**:
  What do you do on weekends?
  I play tennis.
  What do you like in people?
  Kindness.

  Note: a) Negative questions are also used in English.

  Who doesn't understand?
  Luba. She doesn't understand English well.

What doesn't work?
The V.C.R. The picture doesn't come on.

Doesn't the teacher speak French?
Oh yes! Mrs. Shapiro **speaks** *French very well.*
OR: No, Mrs. Shapiro **doesn't speak** *French at all.*

Don't you want any coffee?
No, thank you. I **don't** *drink coffee.*

Note: b) In English, *yes* is always used in an affirmative answer and *no* in a negative answer.

1.5   MORE USES OF *DO*

Do is also used in the following cases.

a)   In idiomatic expressions.

Do *the cleaning*	**Do** *the washing*	**Do** *the baking*
Do *the ironing*	**Do** *the cooking*	**Do** *the shopping*
Do *the work*	**Do** *the laundry*	**Do** *the housework*

b)   In short answers in the simple present tense, to avoid repetition of the verb.

Do you speak English?
Yes, I **do**.

Does he have a dictionary?
No, he **doesn't**.

Do Katia and Ron smoke?
No, they **don't**.

Don't they live here?
Yes, they **do**.

Don't they have a car?
No, they **don't**.

c)   To ask about a person's profession.

What **does** *Eldon* **do**?
He's a teacher.

What **does** *Ning* **do**?
She paints.

What **do** *you* **do**?
I don't work. I go to school.

1.6   SOME USES OF THE SIMPLE PRESENT TENSE

The simple present tense is used in the following cases.

a)   To express customs, habits or certain capabilities.
*Christians **celebrate** Christmas.*
***Do** you **take** sugar in your coffee?*
*We **take** the bus to school.*
*We **go** to school every day.*
*Helmut **speaks** Polish and English.*

b)   To express general statements and truths.
*Children **like** holidays.*
*The sun **rises** in the east.*

1.7   EXPRESSIONS OF FREQUENCY

a)   ***Always**, **usually**, **often**, **sometimes**, **seldom**, **rarely** and **never***
usually express **how often** or **how many times** we do something.
They come before the verb in the simple present tense.

Note: *sometimes* can also be placed at the beginning or at the end of a sentence.

You	ALWAYS USUALLY	take the bus to school.
We	OFTEN SOMETIMES SELDOM	take a taxi.
He	RARELY NEVER	has lunch at home.

Sometimes Rosalia has lunch at school.
Rosalia sometimes has lunch at school.
Rosalia has lunch at school sometimes.

b) The following are expressions of frequency:
once a day, a week, a month, a year
twice (two times) a day, a week, a month, a year
every day, week, month, year
every other (alternating) day, week, month, year
every three (or any number) days, weeks, months, years

These expressions usually come at the end of a sentence.

How often do you go to the movies?
Three times a month. (I go to the movies three times a month.)

How often does he paint the living room?
Every three years. (He paints the living room every three years.)

How many times a week do you do the laundry?
Once a week. (I do the laundry once a week.)

How often does he visit his parents?
Every other weekend. (He visits his parents every other weekend.)

How often does he visit his sister?
Every other weekend. (He visits his sister every other weekend.)

1.8 THE IMPERATIVE

The imperative expresses a command, order or strong request. It is formed with the infinitive and uses the same form for second person singular or plural.

Listen! Look! Repeat, please! Wait! Please be quiet!
Speak English, please! Please, spell your name!

The negative is formed with *don't* + Infinitive.

Don't write now!
Don't smoke here!
Don't chew gum!
Don't open the book yet, please.
Please, don't eat or drink in the classroom.

(See Unit 13 for more on the imperative.)

1.9 PRONUNCIATION OF THE THIRD PERSON SINGULAR

SINGULAR ENDING

The third person singular endings, *s* and *es*, are pronounced /Iz/, /z/ or /s/, depending on the last sound of the infinitive.

a) They are pronounced /Iz/ after infinitives ending in sibilants (/z/, /s/, /dʒ/, /ʒ/, /tʃ/, / ʃ /):
close /kloz/, closes /klozIz/
massage /masaʒ/, massages /masaʒIz/
kiss /kIs/,   kisses /kIsIz/
catch /kætʃ /, catches /kætʃ Iz/
push /pʊʃ /, pushes /pʊʃ Iz/

b) They are pronounced /z/ after infinitives ending in vowel sounds or in voiced consonants other than the sibilants /z/, /dʒ/ and /ʒ/:
show /ʃo/, shows /ʃoz/
go /go/, goes /goz/
carry /kæri/, carries /kæriz/
guide /gaId/, guides /gaIdz/
rain /reIn/, rains /reInz/
sing /sIŋ/, sings /sIŋz/
live /lIv/, lives /lIvz/

c) They are pronounced /s/ after infinitives ending in the consonants (/p/, /t/, /k/ and /f/):
put /pʊt/, puts /pʊts/
keep /kip/, keeps /kips/
walk /wɔk/, walks /wɔks/
sniff /snIf/, sniffs /snIfs/

Note: a) The following pronunciations are irregular:

do /du/, does /dʌz/ (or /dɔz/ when unstressed)
say /seI/, says /sɛz/

   b) The following verb is irregular:

have /hæv/, has /hæz/

1.10 EXERCISES

PRACTICE YOUR PRONUNCIATION

1. Pronounce *es* as /IZ/ in the following words:

she teaches	he washes	he kisses
she catches	she rushes	she crosses
he tosses	he uses	he places
she erases	it freezes	she fixes
he fetches	it closes	he misses

2. Pronounce *s* as /s/ in the following words:

he talks	he walks	she paints
he knocks	she takes	she makes
he mops	it hops	it stops
she shops	It works	he fights
she shouts	it writes	he drinks

3. Pronounce *s* as /Z/ in the following words:

he plays	he prepares	he shaves
she uses	she comes	she wears
he studies	he repairs	he begins
she lives	it sings	he brings
he receives	he believes	he opens
she reads	he draws	it smells
he hears	he cries	she copies

4. Pronounce *do you* as /du ju/ in the following questions:

Do you cook?	Do you bake?
Do you paint?	Do you draw?
Do you knit?	Do you sew?
Do you type?	Do you sing?
Do you dance?	Do you ski?
Do you swim?	Do you skate?

5. Pronounce *does he* as /dʌZ hi/, and *does she* as /dʌZ ʃi/ in the following questions:

Does he cook?	Does he bake?
Does she paint?	Does she draw?
Does she knit?	Does he sew?
Does he type?	Does he sing?
Does he dance?	Does he ski?
Does she swim?	Does she skate?

6. Pronounce *don't* as /dont/ in the following statements:

I don't cook.	I don't bake.
I don't paint.	They don't draw.
They don't knit.	We don't sew.
We don't type.	We don't sing.
You don't dance.	You don't ski.
I don't swim.	They don't skate.

7. Pronounce *doesn't* as /dʌZnt/ in the following statements:

He doesn't cook.	She doesn't bake.
He doesn't paint.	He doesn't draw.
She doesn't knit.	He doesn't sew.
She doesn't type.	She doesn't sing.
He doesn't dance.	He doesn't ski.
She doesn't swim.	She doesn't skate.

IMPROVE YOUR SPEAKING AND WRITING

1. Work with a partner. Your partner and you will take turns telling each other and then writing down your statement. (See 1.1 and 1.2.)
   a) If you like or don't like jazz, ballet, football, opera, movies, hockey.

EXAMPLE: I **like** (or **I don't like**) jazz.   I _____ like (I don't like_ opera.

I _____ like (I don't like_ ballet.   I _____ like (I don't like_ movies.

I _____ football.　I _____ hockey.

b)　If you drink or don't drink wine, lemonade, milk, coffee, beer.

I _____ wine.　I _____ tea.

I _____ lemonade.　I _____ coffee.

I _____ milk.　I _____ beer.

c)　If you play or don't play cards, bridge, chess, tennis, volleyball, soccer.

I _____ cards.　I _____ tennis.

I _____ bridge.　I _____ volleyball.

I _____ chess.　I _____ soccer.

2.　Now tell the class and then write about your partner:
a)　If she or he likes or doesn't like jazz, ballet, football, opera, movies, hockey.

EXAMPLE:　He or she likes (OR doesn't like) jazz.

_____ ballet.　_____ football.

_____ opera.　_____ movies.

_____ hockey.

b)　If she or he drinks (or doesn't drink) wine, lemonade, milk, tea, coffee, beer.

_____ wine.　_____ tea.

_____ lemonade.　_____ coffee.

_____ milk.　_____ beer.

c)　If she or he plays (OR doesn't play) cards, bridge, chess, tennis, volleyball, soccer.

_____ poker.　_____ tennis.

_____ bridge.　_____ volleyball.

_____ chess.　_____ soccer.

3.　Ask a partner about the following activities. Your partner will respond. Write down both the answers and the questions. (See 1.3.)

	You ask:	Your partner answers:
EXAMPLE:	(draw) **Do you draw?**	**Yes, I do** OR **No, I don't.**

	You ask:		Your partner answers:
	(paint) _____ ?		_____ .
	(dance) _____ ?		_____ .
	(play cards) _____ ?		_____ .
	(drink coffee) _____ ?		_____ .
	(eat hot dogs) _____ ?		_____ .
	(wear jeans) _____ ?		_____ .
	(watch the news) _____ ?		_____ .

4. Now tell the class and then write about your partner, using Exercise 3 above.

EXAMPLE: (Name of partner) **draws** (or **doesn't draw**).

(paint) _____ .

(dance) _____ .

(play cards) _____ .

(drink coffee) _____ .

(eat hot dogs) _____ .

(wear jeans) _____ .

(watch the news) _____ .

5. Interview your partner about a friend or family member.

	You ask:	Your partner answers:
EXAMPLE:	(draw) **Does** (name) **draw?**	**Yes, he/she does.** OR **No, he/she doesn't.**

	You ask:		Your partner answers:
	(paint) _____ ?		_____ .
	(dance) _____ ?		_____ .
	(play cards) _____ ?		_____ .
	(drink coffee) _____ ?		_____ .
	(eat hot dogs) _____ ?		_____ .
	(wear jeans) _____ ?		_____ .
	(watch the news) _____ ?		_____ .

6. Make an affirmative or negative statement about yourself.

EXAMPLE: (study English) **I study English.**

(speak Cantonese) _____ .

(speak Spanish) _____ .

(understand French) _____ .

(have a job) _____ .

(have a car) _____ .

(play basketball) _____ .

(like music) _____ .

(watch T.V.) _____ .

(drink wine) _____ .

(eat hamburgers) _____ .

(wear make-up) _____ .

(play tennis) _____ .

7. Repeat Exercise 6, but tell and write about a family member.

EXAMPLE: (Name) **studies/or doesn't study English.**

(speak Cantonese) _____ .

(speak Spanish) _____ .

(understand French) _____ .

(have a job) _____ .

(have a car) _____ .

(play basketball) _____ .

(like music) _____ .

(watch T.V.) _____ .

(drink wine) _____ .

(eat hamburgers) _____ .

(wear make-up) _____ .

(play tennis) _____ .

8. Complete the following sentences with a form of *do*.

EXAMPLE: **Do** you like jam?
             No, I **don't**.

a) _____ the teacher speak French?

No, he _____ .

_____ he understand French at all?

No, he _____ .

_____ he use the dictionary?

Sometimes he _____ .

b) _____ you wear jeans?

Yes, I _____ , but my brother _____ .

_____ your sister wear shorts?

In the summer, she _____ .

c) _____ you enjoy opera?

Yes, _____ , but I prefer jazz.

_____ Massoud like reggae music? No, he

_____ .

d) _____ you like classical music? No, I _____ .

_____ you like rap music? No, I _____ .

_____ you enjoy jazz music? No, I _____ .

_____ you like music? I _____ , but I prefer movies.

e) We dance the tango, but we _____ dance the polka.

_____ you dance the polka?

I _____ , but Loretta _____ .

f) Who _____ the laundry?

My sister _____ .

Who _____ the cooking?

My brother _____ .

Who _____ the house cleaning?

My sister and my brother _____ .

What _____ you _____ ?

I _____ the dishes.

g) Who makes breakfast in the morning?

I _____ .

Who makes dinner?

My sister _____ .

9. Work with a partner. Your partner will create questions that ask for the italicized information. He or she will use *who, what* or *when.* (See 1.4.)

EXAMPLE: They read *books.* **What do they read?**

a) *water* freezes at 0°C. _____

b) They wear *uniforms* to school. _____

c) Pedro and Maria speak *Spanish.* _____

d) David *plays bridge* every Sunday. _____

e) *George and Betty* paint and draw. _____

f) Rita *visits friends* on Sundays. _____

g) Grandpa and Grandma watch *films on T.V.*

h) They like *fish.* _____

i) Ecuador grows *vegetables.* _____

j) I visit my parents *every weekend.* _____

k) She does the shopping *every Saturday.* _____

l) Mexico exports *fruit.* _____

m) Canada imports *computers.* _____

n) Paul exports *wood.* _____

10. Complete each of the following sentences with the correct form of the verb provided.

EXAMPLE: Mona **plays** (play) the piano and Magdi **sings** (sing).

a) Bob and Sylvia (not live) _____don't live_____ here.

b) The Smiths (not know) _____ the Clarks and the

Clarks (not know) _____ the Smiths.

17

c) Grandfather (not work) _He_ _doesn't work_ . He (stay)s
_____ home.

d) Grandmother (work) _____ part-time. She (teach)
_____ geography.

e) Margarita, please (do) _____ the exercise, (not
read) _____ the magazine!

f) José, please (spell) _____ your family name.

g) Mr. Chow, _____ you (have) _____ an
appointment?
Yes, I do.
All right, please (hang) _____ up your coat and
(take) _____ a seat.

h) Pratima (swim) _____ . Ishwar doesn't. He (skate)
_____ .

i) Roberta and Draga usually (play) _____ basketball
on Sundays.

j) Ying (work) _____ and Tang (go) _____
to university.

k) Rosa (paint) _____ and her husband (make)
_____ pottery.

l) _____ Tonay and Gina (understand) _____
the instructions?

m) Mary (love) _____ Rob but Rob (love) _____
Anita.

n) "Your Friendly Dairy" (make) _____ and (sell)
_____ ice cream.

o) What _____ Sonia (do) _____ ?
She (sort) _____ and (deliver) _____
the mail.

p) Do you (drink) _____ beer with your meals?

No, I _____ . I always (have) _____
water or Chinese tea.

q) _____ Samir (bake) _____ bread?
No, but he usually (bake) _____ a cake on Sundays.

r) _____ you (see) _____ Rita every week?
No, I usually (see) _____ her at the club every second week.

s) _____ you sometimes (try) _____ new food?
Very seldom. I (prefer) _____ Greek food. I almost
always (eat) _____ Greek food. But sometimes I
(have) _____ Chinese food. My sister always (try)
_____ new food.

t) Please (be) _____ quiet! (Do) _____ your
exercise. Then (read) _____ the assignment. (Not talk)
_____ .

u) Miguel (teach) _____ Spanish. I (teach) _____
Portuguese.

v) I (love) _____ Aunt Celia. I (call) _____ Aunt
Celia once a week.

w) _____ Mr. Gonzales (speak) _____ Russian?
He (understand) _____ Russian but (not speak)
_____ it.

11. The following sentences are in the imperative. Complete them in
your own words. (See 1.8.)

EXAMPLE: Sucheta! Please **don't run** in the house.

a) Sam! Please, _____ play ball in the house.

b) Please, don't _____ late tomorrow.

c) Please, _____ your name.

d) _____ your name here, please.

e) _____ your dinner! Don't _____ .

f) Don't _____ gum in the classroom.

g) Don't _____ or _____ in the classroom.

h) Please, _____ smoke here.

i) _____ the story, then _____ the questions.

j) Laura! Don't _____ your brother!

k) _____ talk! _____ your exercises!

l) Don't _____ the dishes now! _____ your homework first.

m) _____ some milk, then _____ to bed.

n) _____ your face, _____ your teeth and then _____ to bed.

12. This is a conversation between Rachel and Khalis. Work with a partner. Create the missing questions for Rachel. Then write down the information. (See 1.7.)

EXAMPLE: R: **How often do you paint the house?**

K: Every four years.

R: **How often do you clean your house?**

K: Once a week.

a) R: _How often do you work in house_ ?

K: Yes, it works well.

R: _____ ?

K: It mixes paints.

b) R: _____ ?

K: My wife does.

R: _____ ?

K: Well, yes, my wife does the shopping, but I do the cooking.

c) R: _____ ?

K: Every other weekend.

R: _____ ?

K: Oh, every day!

d) R: _How often do you drink beer_ ?
K: Once a day.
R: _How often do you go to shopping_ ?
K: Once a week.

e) R: _____ ?
K: No, she drives a truck.
R: _____ ?
K: No, she flies a helicopter.

f) R: _____ ?
K: About once a month.
R: _____ ?
K: Oh, I buy milk once a week.

g) R: _____ ?
K: I usually stay home.
R: _____ ?
K: Sometimes we visit friends, sometimes we stay home.

h) R: _____ ?
K: No, he plays bridge.
R: _How often do you play bingo_ ?
K: Every Sunday.

i) R: _____ ?
K: No, but I like duck.
R: _____ ?
K: Once every two months.

j) R: _____ ?
K: No, he doesn't.
R: _____ ?
K: He works.

13. **What are these people saying? Follow the example.**

EXAMPLE: A: How often do you speak French?

B: Never. I never speak French.

a)   A: _How many times do you go do Shopping_

B: Once a week.

b)   A: _How often do you play bingo_

B: Never. _I never play bingo_

c)   A: _How often do you drink beer_

B: Rarely. _I drink beer._

d)   A: _How often do you watch television_

B: Every day.

e)   A: _How often do you cook a roast_

B: Every two weeks.

f)   A: _How often do you have parties_

B: Seldom.

g)   A: _How often do you eat chicken_

B: Every three days.

h)   A: _How often do you eat popcorn_

B: Twice a week.

i)   A: _How often do you exercise_

B: Every Saturday.

j)   A: _How often do you visit neighbours_

B: Once a month.

14. **This is a conversation between Xiang and Ying. Work with a partner. Create the missing questions using the suggested verbs. Then write down the information.**

EXAMPLE: (have)   X: **Do you have any pets?**
Y: Yes, a dog and a cat.

(fight)   X: **Do they fight?**
Y: Sometimes they do.

a) (exercise) X: _____ ?

                Y: Three times a week.

    (do) X: _____ ?

                Y: I run.

    (play) X: _____ ?

                Y: I do, but I prefer football.

b) (like) X: _____ gardening?

                Y: Fatima.

    (grow) X: _____ ?

                Y: Roses and tulips.

c) (run) X: _____ the office?

                Y: No, she doesn't.

    (manage) X: _____ ?

                Y: She manages the warehouse.

d) (drink) X: _____ ?

                Y: I always drink tea.

    (have coffee) X: _____ ?

                Y: Sometimes I do.

e) (know) X: _____ Carlos?

                Y: Yes, I do.

    (do) X: _____ ?

                Y: He sells insurance.

f) (make) X: _____ jewelry?

                Y: Mr. Nguyen does.

    (use) X: _____ ?

                Y: Gold and silver.

g) (do) X: _____ ?

                Y: He paints.

    X: _____ ?

    Y: Children.

15. Copy the chart below in your notebook.

a) Fill in the first line of the chart (the one that begins with I). Under each activity, mark a U if you do this activity, and an x if you don't.

b) Interview three people. Ask them if they do these activities. Mark each square with a U or an x depending on their answers.

c) Tell the class about you and your three partners.

EXAMPLE: I don't ski but I swim. I cook and I sew. I don't play the guitar. I don't play tennis. I skate but I don't ski.

Monika skis and swims....

	Ski	Swim	Cook	Sew	Play the guitar	Play tennis	Skate	Ski
I								
(name)								
(name)								
(name)								

EXPRESS YOURSELF

1. Ask a partner the following questions. Your partner will answer. Then ask three questions of your own, and write your questions down.

   a) What do you usually do on Sundays?

   b) What do you usually do on Saturdays?

   c) What do you sometimes do on Fridays?

   d) When do you have a family get-together?

   e) When do you do the laundry?

   f) How often do you make chow mein?

   g) How often do you entertain?

   h) How often do you play music?

   i) How often do you watch T.V.?

j)   When do you watch T.V.?

k)   In your home, who does the cleaning?

l)   In your home, who makes the breakfast?

m)   In your home, who prepares dinner?

n)   In your home, who does the dishes?

o)   In your home, who studies English?

2.   Ask a partner the following questions. Your partner will answer in complete statements.

a)   How often does it rain in the desert?

b)   How often does the sun shine in the desert?

c)   How often does it snow in Cuba?

d)   How often does it rain in Cuba?

e)   How often does it snow in Vancouver?

f)   How often does it rain in Vancouver?

3.   Ask a partner the following questions. Your partner will answer in short statements. Then ask three questions of your own, and write your questions down.

a)   Do you write poetry?

b)   Do you practice English every day?

c)   Do you like reggae music?

d)   Do you travel on weekends?

e)   Do you enjoy politics?

f)   Do you exercise?

g)   Do you practice music?

h)   Who cleans the classroom?

i)   Who runs the school?

j)   Who celebrates Christmas?

k)   Who celebrates Eid Fetr (Ramadan)?

l)   Who celebrates Hanukkah?

m)   When do you visit friends?

n)   When do you have snacks?

UNIT 2 – PLURAL FORM OF NOUNS AND DETERMINERS

2.1 COUNTABLE NOUNS

Countable nouns represent things that we can count. They are used in the singular or plural form.

*I have a **dog**.*　　　　　　　　*She has three **dogs**.*
*She uses a **pencil**.*　　　　　　*She uses two **pencils**.*

2.2 REGULAR PLURAL FORMS

In general, add *s* to the noun to form the plural.

table, **tables**	*hand,* **hands**	*picture,* **pictures**
wall, **walls**	*pencil,* **pencils**	*pen,* **pens**

EXCEPTIONS TO THE GENERAL RULE

a)　Add *es* to *s, sh, ch* or *x* endings.

　　boss, **bosses**　　　　　　　　*match,* **matches**
　　brush, **brushes**　　　　　　　*box,* **boxes**

Exception: When *ch* is pronounced *k*, add *s*.
　　　　　　　stomach, **stomachs**

b)　Add *es* to *o* endings.

　　tomato, **tomatoes**　　　　　　*potato,* **potatoes**

Exception: When the noun is related to music, add *s*.
　　　　　　　soprano, **sopranos**　　piano, **pianos**

c)　Change *f* or *fe* endings to *ves*.

　　wife, **wives**　　　　　　　　*shelf,* **shelves**

Exceptions:
　　chief, **chiefs**　　　　　roof, **roofs**
　　handkerchief, **handkerchiefs**

d)　Change *y* ending to *ies*.

　　lady, **ladies**
　　cherry, **cherries**

2.3 IRREGULAR PLURAL FORMS

a) The following nouns have no plural form.

*One deer, four **deer***   *one salmon, six **salmon***
*One fish, three **fish***   *one sheep, three **sheep***
*One moose, two **moose***

b) The following nouns change in the plural, but have an irregular plural form.

*One foot, two **feet***   *one woman, many **women***
*One mouse, three **mice***   *one child, nine **children***
*One tooth, three **teeth***

c) In compound nouns, the more important word usually changes in the plural.

*A mother-in-law, all **mothers-in-law***
*A governor general, **the governors general***

2.4 UNCOUNTABLE NOUNS

Uncountable nouns represent a concept, an abstract word or something that we cannot count. Uncountable nouns have no plural.
*We don't like **violence**.*
*They don't have **electricity**.*
*Do they drink **wine**?*
*Does she need **help**?*
*She doesn't eat **bread**.*

2.5 PLURAL OF UNCOUNTABLE NOUNS

Uncountable nouns have no plural. Here are a few examples:

advice	*bread*	*food*	*information*
cheese	*fruit*	*work*	*wine*
water	*duty*	*beer*	*liquid*
mail	*art*	*glass*	*money*
sculpture	*gold*	*paper*	*religion*
silver	*butter*	*steak*	*wood*

Some uncountable nouns can be used as countable nouns but with a different meaning. The plural usually refers to different kinds of the noun, or the number of units of the noun.

He likes coffee.	**Two coffees**, please. *(two cups)*
I enjoy art.	I enjoy **folk arts**. *(different forms of art)*
She loves steak.	She buys **four steaks** a week. *(four portions)*
They love sculpture.	They own **three Rodin sculptures**. *(three pieces of a particular artist's sculpture)*
We don't discuss religion in class.	They study **the religions of the world**. *(the different kinds of religion)*
I love cheese and wine.	The store sells **cheeses and wines from all over the world**. *(different kinds)*
I don't eat lamb.	They have **two lambs**.
He drinks beer.	He drinks **three beers** a day. *(three bottles of beer)*

2.6 DETERMINERS

Determiners are mainly:

* articles (**a**, **an**, **the**)
* cardinal numbers (**one**, **two**, **three**, etc.)
* words of count and measure such as **some**, **no**, **any**, or **a few**, **many**, **several** (see Unit 3)
* the possessive and demonstrative adjectives (see Unit 5)

2.7 THE INDEFINITE ARTICLES, *A* AND *AN*

The indefinite articles **a** and **an** are used before a countable noun when it represents no particular person or thing.

I need *a radio*. *(no particular radio)*
She wants *an apple*. *(no particular apple)*

A is used before a singular noun beginning with a consonant, or a vowel with a sound like a consonant.

a child, a door, a university, a union, a home, a hotel

An is used before a singular noun beginning with a vowel or a silent *h*.

an egg, an hour, an onion, an apple

A or *an* is dropped in the plural form.

They sell radios.
They import cars.
We love children.

Note: *One* is used in contrast with *two* or *three*.

How many brothers and sisters does she have?
*She has **one** brother and three sisters.*

The indefinite article is used in an ordinary statement.

Does she have any siblings?
*She has **a** brother and three sisters.*

2.8   THE DEFINITE ARTICLE, *THE*

The definite article **the** is used when the noun represents a particular person or thing.

*I like **the** new table in **the** conference room. (a particular table in a special room)*

The is used to represent the only person or object in the world or in a certain place.

***The** sun gives light. (only one sun in the world)*
*I know **the** mayor of Toronto. (only one mayor)*

The is the same for the singular and the plural.

*We like **the** new park. We like **the** parks in Saskatoon.*

The is **not** used before countries, towns, cities, proper nouns and proper nouns with a title.

Exceptions:
a)   Use *the* before the names of countries with a plural form.

The Netherlands   *The* Philippines
The Netherlands do not produce bananas. What do *the* Philippines export?

b) Use *the* before the name of countries that include *United, Republic of,* or *Kingdom of.*
the United States
the Republic of China
the United Kingdom
Scotland is part of **the** *United Kingdom.*
Chi-Keung visits **the** *Republic of China every five years.*

c) The only city used with *the* is The Hague in the Netherlands.
Eric Leeman comes from **the Hague**.

2.9 *SOME/ANY/NO*

Some and **any** mean a certain quantity. They are used with or without a noun.
Some is used in affirmative statements and in questions where a *yes* answer is expected.

I need **some** *flour and some eggs.*
Mary needs some too.

Do you want **some** *tea?*
Yes, please.

Do you need **some** *extra folders?*
Yes, about three, please.

Any is used in negative or interrogative sentences.
I don't need **any** *flour.*
Do you need **any** *eggs?*
Yes, I need **some***./No, I don't need* **any***.*

No means *not any*. It is used with a noun.
She has **no** *time.*
I have **no** *money.*

Some, any and *no* are used to form the following words: **someone, somebody, anyone, anybody, no one** and **nobody** for people, and **something, anything** and **nothing** for things. These words follow the same rules as *some, any* and *no*.

*Do you know **anyone** here?*
*No, **no one**. I don't know **anyone/anybody** here.*

*You look tired. Do you need **anything**?*
*No, thank you. I don't need **anything**.*

*Do you need **something** from the supermarket?*
*Yes, I need **some** rice.*

*Does **anybody** here speak Swahili?*
*No, **nobody** does.*

*Do you need **something** to eat?*
*No, thank you. I don't need **anything**.*

*Do you need **somebody** for the computer room?*
*No, we don't need **anybody** yet.*

2.10 PRONUNCIATION OF THE PLURAL FORMS OF NOUNS AND DETERMINERS

REGULAR PLURAL ENDINGS

The regular plural endings *s* and *es* are pronounced /Iz/, /z/ or /s/, depending on the last sound of the noun.

a) They are pronounced /Iz/ after nouns ending in sibilants (/s/, /s/, /dʒ/, /ʒ/, /tʃ/, /ʃ/).

nose	/noz/,	*noses*	/nowzIz/
house	/haus/,	*houses*	/hausIz/
bridge	/brIdʒ/,	*bridges*	/brIdʒIz/
mirage	/mIraʒ/,	*mirages*	/mIraʒIz/
church	/tʃɜtʃ/,	*churches*	/tʃɜtʃIz/
dish	/dIʃ/,	*dishes*	/dIʃIz/

b) They are pronounced /z/ after nouns ending in vowel sounds or in voiced consonants other than the sibilants /z/, /dʒ/, /ʒ/.

piano	/pjæno/,	*pianos*	/pjænoz/
torpedo	/tɔrpIdo/,	*torpedos*	/tɔrpIdoz/
berry	/bɛri/,	*berries*	/bɛriz/
cab	/kæb/,	*cabs*	/kæbz/
bed	/bɛd/,	*beds*	/bɛdz/

dog	/dɔg/,	dogs	/dɔgz/
home	/hom/,	homes	/homz/
can	/kæn/,	cans	/kænz/
ball	/bɔl/,	balls	/bɔlz/
car	/kar/,	cars	/karz/

c) They are pronounced /s/ after nouns ending in the consonants /p/, /t/, /k/, /f/.

map	/mæp/,	maps	/mæps/
cat	/kæt/,	cats	/kæts/
cook	/kʊk/,	cooks	/kʊks/
roof	/ruf/,	roofs	/rufs/
cough	/kɔf/,	cough	/kɔfs/

Note: The following nouns are pronounced differently in the singular and in the plural.

foot	/fʊt/,	feet	/fit/
man	/mæn/,	men	/mɛn/
woman	/wʊmʌn/,	women	/wImIn/
mouse	/maus/,	mice	/maIs/
ox	/ɔks/,	oxen	/ɔksIn/
tooth	/tuθ/,	teeth	/tiθ/
child	/tʃaIld/,	children	/tʃIldrIn/

THE DEFINITE ARTICLE, *THE*

The definite article, *the*, is pronounced /ð/ before a consonant sound, /ʒI/ before a vowel sound and /ð/ when it is stressed and means "the best, the famous".

the book	/ðə bʊk/	the egg	/ðI ɛg/
the shop	/ðə ʃɔp/	the owl	/ðI aʊl/
She is **the** greatest living singer!		.../ði/ greatest living singer!	
He is **the** Liberace.		.../ði/ Liberace.	

THE INDEFINITE ARTICLES, *A* AND *AN*

A is pronounced /ʌ/.

bag	/ʌ/ bag
mat	/ʌ/ mat
lock	/ʌ/ lock

hill　　　　　/ʌ/ *hill*
machine　　　/ʌ/ *machine*

An is pronounced /æn/.
ocean　　　/æn/ *ocean*
arm　　　　/æn/ *arm*
office　　　/æn/ *office*
artist　　　/æn/ *artist*
address　　/æn/ *address*

2.11　EXERCISES

PRACTICE YOUR PRONUNCIATION

1.　a)　Pronounce *the* as /ðə/ with the following words:
　　　　the hat, the child, the home, the box, the coffee, the cream, the paper,
　　　　the meat, the goose, the park, the houses, the matches, the pictures,
　　　　the flower, the man

　　b)　Pronounce *the* to rhyme with *he* or *she* with the following
　　　　words:
　　　　the army, the ashtray, the actors, the eye, the eggs, the animal,
　　　　the oven, the ocean, the orange, the olive, the offices, the apartments,
　　　　the hours, the ox, the exercises, the end, the answers, the air,
　　　　the objects, the afternoon

2.　a)　Pronounce *a* as / ʌ / with the following words:
　　　　a wallet, a purse, a briefcase, a notebook, a grammar text, a workbook,
　　　　a manual, a picnic, a zoo, a garden, a forest, a magazine, a newspaper,
　　　　a brochure, a dime, a nickel, a dollar, a portrait, a film, a gate, a carpet,
　　　　a sandwich, a basket, a counter, a fence

　　b)　Pronounce *an* as / æ n/ with the following words:
　　　　an earring, an ear, an uncle, an aunt, an inch, an ounce, an antenna,
　　　　an airplane, an airport, an hour, an aquarium, an idea, an interview,
　　　　an afternoon, an evening, an arm, an elbow, an index, an admirer,
　　　　an ox, an identification, an educator, an invitation, an apple

IMPROVE YOUR SPEAKING AND WRITING

1. Write the plural form of the following singular nouns. (See 2.2 and 2.3.)

EXAMPLE: pencil, **pencils**

book	books	lamp	lamps
goose	geese	watch	whacles
tree	trees	box	boxes
farm	farms	ox	ox
housekeeper	housekeepers	tooth	teeth
mouse	Mouse	glass	glasses
chicken	chicken	lamb	
child	children	watch	watches
brother-in-law	brother-in-laws	foot	feet
man	men	woman	women
ship	ship	barber	barbers
desk	desks	store	stores
university	universiti	tomato	tomatoes
soprano		leaf	
fellow		wife	wife
roof	roofs	shelf	
library	libraries	brush	brushes
radio	radios	deer	deer
fish	fishes	bird	birds
cherry	cherries	kiss	kii
chief	chief		

2. A child asks you questions about animals. You will answer by making an affirmative or negative statement with each noun. Use the suggested verb.

EXAMPLE: Airplanes **fly**.

Elephants **do not fly**.

a) crawl

    Mice

    Snakes

    A fox

    A worm

b) hop

    Kangaroos

    Frogs

    A dog

    Chickens

c) run

    Turtle

    A deer

    Rabbits

    An ant

d) swim

    Fish

    A salmon

    Sheep

    An ox

e) bite

    Mosquitoes

    Squirrels

    A spider

    A beetle

f) sting

    Bees

    Flies

    A butterfly

    A wasp

g) purr

    Cats

    Tigers

    A hamster

    A monkey

h) eat meat

    Pandas

    Pigeons

    Owls

    A loon

3. Work with a partner. You and your partner will take turns telling each other and then writing down what each of the following people does. Use more than one verb when possible.

EXAMPLE: **A hairdresser cuts, styles and trims hair.**

a) A shoemaker

b) A hockey player

c) A housekeeper

d) A mail carrier

e) A mechanic

f) A salesperson

g) A secretary

h) A cook

i) A painter

j) A dressmaker

k) A baker

l) A dentist

4. Work with a partner. You and your partner will take turns telling

each other and then writing down what each of the following stores sells. Use more than one object. (See 2.5.)

EXAMPLE: A computer **store sells computers and computer books**.

a) A drugstore

b) A variety store

c) A milk store

d) A shoe store

e) A hardware store

f) A pet shop

g) A supermarket

h) A furniture store

i) A department store

j) A nursery

k) A bookstore

l) A gift shop

5. Complete the following conversations with *a, an, one* or *the* where necessary. (See 2.7 and 2.8.)

a) What does Michael do?

He builds _____ fireplaces.

How many stores does he manage?

Just _____ .

What does he drive?

_____ a _____ truck.

Who does he usually contact?

_____ the _____ customers.

b) What do you study?

_____ the _____ medicine.

Do you take _____ biology?

I do.

How often do you work in _____ the _____ lab?

Five times _____ week.

c) Class, what does _____ map show?

_____ *the* _____ Nile River and _____ Pyramids.

Does _____ *the* _____ Nile flow through _____ *the* _____ Libya?

No, it flows through _____ *an* _____ Egypt and _____ *the* _____ Sudan.

What do you call _____ White Nile? _____ river or branch?

_____ branch or _____ tributary.

d) Who is Mary dating? _____ *the an* _____ accountant?

Oh no! She's seeing _____ *a* _____ writer now.

What does he write?

_____ plays. He also teaches _____ *a* _____ poetry.

e) Do you have _____ *some* _____ children?

Yes, _____ *I have* _____ .

Do you have _____ *a* _____ boy or _____ *a* _____ girl?

_____ *the* _____ boy.

Does he like school?

Yes, he loves _____ teacher and he enjoys math and

_____ *an* _____ English, but he doesn't enjoy sports. He prefers

_____ *some* _____ crafts and _____ *the* _____ music.

f) I need _____ *a* _____ desk, _____ *an* _____ armchair and

_____ *a* _____ lamp. I don't see any desks or _____ *any* _____

armchairs here, just _____ lamps.

Please follow me to _____ *the* _____ other room. Do you need any kitchen chairs?

No, *don't need* _____ kitchen chairs just _____ *the* _____ armchair.

6. What are these people saying? Follow the example.

EXAMPLE: A: What do you drink in the morning?

B: I drink tea.

a)   A: _____ eat at lunch?

B: _____

b)   A: _____ cook on Fridays?

B: _____

c)   A: _____ have for a snack?

B: _____

d)   A: _____ drink at supper?

B: _____

e)   A: _____ order at McDonald's?

B: _____

f)   A: _____ prepare for friends?

B: _____

g)   A: _____ take on a picnic?

B: _____

h)   A: _____ buy at Donut World?

B: _____

i)   A: _____ store in your freezer?

B: _____

j)   A: _____ get from Laura Secord?

B: _____

7.   Complete the following sentences using the words provided in either the singular or plural form. Add *some*, *any*, *no*, *a*, *an* or *the* where necessary. (See 2.9.)

Example: How often do you rent **movies** (movies)?

We never rent **any movies** (movies). We just watch **the news** (news) on T.V.

a) Do you shorten _____ (pants)?

Yes, we do. We also alter _____ (dress).

b) Is there _____ (hole) in _____ (tights)?

No, there isn't _____ (hole) but there's _____ (run).

c) I admire _____ (courage), Bob, but I prefer _____ (caution).

d) Would you like _____ (soup)? No, I don't want _____ (soup) but I would like _____ (broccoli).

e) Who do _____ (teenager) usually imitate? They imitate _____ (actor) and _____ (model).

f) Does Helga paint _____ (portrait)?

No, she doesn't paint _____ (portrait). She draws _____ (animals).

g) _____ (Money) doesn't buy _____ (happiness).

h) Do you have _____ (appointment), Ms. Ellis?

No, I don't have one, but I need to see _____ (doctor) today.

All right, please take _____ (seat).

8. Complete the following sentences using the word provided in the singular or plural form. (See 2.5.)

EXAMPLE: I like **chicken** (chicken).

I have two **chickens** (chicken) in the freezer.

a) My grandfather raises _____ (rabbit).

b) We eat a lot of _____ (rabbit).

c) Roger and I don't like _____ (steak).

d) I want two T-bone _____ (steak), please.

e) We have about four _____ (roast), eight _____ (steak) and a little _____ (chicken) in the freezer.

f) We don't eat _____ (meat) but we love
    _____ (seafood).

g) We drink a lot of _____ (juice). We always have a
    choice of _____ (juice) in the fridge.

h) Do you like _____ (yogurt)?
    Yes, a lot! I eat about two _____ (yogurt) a day.

i) A student uses a lot of _____ (paper).

j) I write about three _____ (papers) a year.

k) What does he do?
    He studies _____ (art).

l) This building contains important _____ (work) of
    _____ (art).

m) Lili works at a centre for the _____ (art).

n) I have a bad back, so I can't do much _____ (work).

o) In theology, we study the different _____ (religion).

p) Mrs. Nuzhat doesn't discuss _____ (religion) or politics
    in class.

9. Write questions for the following answers. If you use *some* in
    your question, explain its use. (See 2.9.)

EXAMPLE: **Do you need some information?**
          Yes, I need some information.

a) No, I don't have any paper.

    _____

b) No, he doesn't study anything.

    _____

c) Yes, someone does the recording.

    _____

d) Yes, the police suspect someone.

    _____

e) No, she doesn't tell the truth.

    _____

f)   No, he doesn't help anyone.

_____

g)   Yes, I do. I hear a motorbike.

_____

h)   Yes, I want some. I love cheese.

_____

i)   Yes, some do. Some juices contain sugar.

_____

j)   No, no one does. No one uses the photocopy machine here.

_____

10. The following are short dialogues between Amr and Boris. Using your own words, create the missing questions and answers.

EXAMPLE: Amr: **What does Ava do?**

Boris: She's a mail carrier. She delivers mail.

Amr: **How often do you get mail?**

Boris: Once a day.

a)   A: _____ ?

B: He farms the land.

A: _____ ?

B: Wheat and vegetables.

A: _____ ?

B: He grows tomatoes.

b)   A: _____ ?

B: They fill cavities and fix teeth.

A: _____ ?

B: Once every six months.

c)   A: Do you read the newspaper?

B: No, I _____. _____ ?

A: Yes, _____ .

B: _____ do you read the newspaper?

A: Every weekend.

42

d)   A: _____?

B: Yes, I do, I know Rocco well.

A: _____?

B: He sells cosmetics.

e)   A: _____?

B: I need some cereal.

A: _____?

B: No, we don't have any.

f)   A: _____?

B: He practices the piano.

A: _____?

B: Every other week.

g)   A: _____?

B: My parents-in-law.

A: _____?

B: They sell land, farms and cottages.

11. Rewrite each of the following sentences using *any*.

EXAMPLE: He has no worries.

He doesn't have any worries.

a)   Mr. Zee has no friends.

b)   He has no pets.

c)   He visits no one.

d)   He has no visitors.

e)   He calls no one.

f)   He gets no calls.

g)   He gets no mail.

h)   He sends no letters.

i)   He sees no one.

j)   He has no plans.

k)   He has no interests.

l)   He has no hobbies.

12. What are these people saying? Follow the example.

EXAMPLE:

A: I need a chicken, a roast of beef and a turkey.

B: We have no turkeys but we have chickens and roasts.

a)

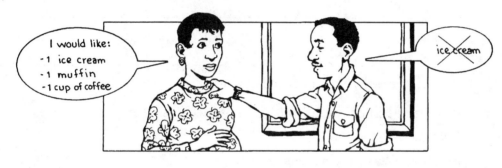

A: _____

B: _____

b)

A: _____

B: _____

c)

A: _____

B: _____

d)

A: _____

B: _____

e)

A: _____

B: _____

EXPRESS YOURSELF

1. Ask a partner the following questions. Your partner will answer. Then ask three questions of your own, and write them down.

    a) Do you understand French?

    b) Do you understand any other languages?

    c) How often do you take time off?

    d) Do you do any typing? Any painting? Any sewing?

    e) Do you know any writers? Any movie stars?

    f) Do you have any pets?

    g) Do you take any courses?

    h) Do you take any medicine?

    i) Do you take showers or baths?

    j) Do you use a calculator?

    k) Do you use the dictionary?

    l) How often do you see the dentist?

    m) How often do you eat a hot dog?

    n) How often do you have a test?

    o) How often do you receive a cheque?

    p) How often do you watch a movie?

    q) How often do you visit the museum?

2. a) Open your fridge. Tell the class what you see.
    b) Look around the room. What furniture do you see? Tell the class.
    c) What furniture do you have in your bedroom? In your living room? Tell a partner.

UNIT 3 – ADJECTIVES

3.1   DESCRIPTIVE ADJECTIVES

Adjectives modify nouns. They are used to describe nouns and tell about size, shape, quantity, quality, length and colour. They usually come before the noun and are always singular.

a **good** car	the **round** table	**wide** streets
the **blue** shirts	a **long** story	some **pretty** flowers

ORDER OF MODIFIERS

When two or more adjectives precede a noun, they are placed in the following order:

1	2	3	4
Determiners	Quality	Size/Height/Length	Age/Temperature
a, an, the	good	little	cold
some	sweet	tall	young
three	wide	long	warm

5	6	7	8
Shape	Colour	Origin/Nationality	Material
square	yellow	Swiss	cotton
round	black	Italian	crystal
oval	green	Greek	silk

a cute little brown dog	a large red silk scarf
a fine old building	an expensive square table
two tall Italian crystal vases	some cold sliced Hungarian sausage

Note: When two or more adjectives come before a noun, only two adjectives of colour or material can be joined with and.

a blue and white cotton dress
a cotton and polyester shirt

3.2 NOUNS USED AS ADJECTIVES

A noun can be used to modify another noun. In such a case, it comes before the noun, and, like the adjective, is always singular.

two **carrot** cakes   five **apple** trees   a **chicken** farm

A noun is used as an adjective in the following cases:

a) When it signifies belonging to some place or environment
   *a **dining room** table*   *the **kitchen** door*

b) When it is the name of a city or town
   *the **Paris** buses*   *the **Vancouver** symphony*

c) When it is related to seasons
   ***summer** sports*   ***winter** games*
   ***spring** flowers*   ***autumn** leaves*

d) When it indicates sports or clothing
   *a **tennis** ball*   *a **golf** course*   *a **football** game*
   ***hockey** sweaters*   *a **coat** lining*   *a **shirt** collar*

e) When it indicates price or cost
   *a **five-dollar** cap*   *a **million-dollar** house*

   Note: Double adjectives (*five-doll*ar cap) are often joined with a hyphen.

f) When it indicates size, measurement or volume
   *a **five-litre** bottle*   *an **eight-lane** highway*

   Note: Watch for the difference between plural nouns and nouns and nouns used as adjectives.

Little Nicole is 95 centimetres tall.
They need three bedrooms.

In these two sentences, *centimetres* and *bedrooms* are plural nouns. But in the next two sentences, *centimetre* and *apartment* are nouns used as adjectives, and are therefore singular.

Little Nicole is a 95-centimetre tall girl.
They need a three-bedroom apartment.

3.3   INFORMATION QUESTIONS WITH *WHAT KIND OF*

What kind of asks for a description of people or things. The *of* is dropped when the noun is omitted.

> *What kind of cookies do you like?*
> Chocolate chip.

> *What kind does Ruth like?*
> Peanut butter.

> *What kind of car does Henry drive?*
> A Pontiac.

> *What kind do you drive?*
> A Buick.

3.4   QUESTIONS WITH *WHICH* AND *WHAT*

a)   **Which** asks about one or more persons or items in a particular group.

> *Which student comes from Brazil, Joanna or Lorella?*
> Lorella.

> *Which student needs a room, Kamala or Kim?*
> Kamala.

b)   **Which one** (singular) and **which ones** (plural) are used to avoid repetition of the noun.

> *Which vase does Helen want?*
> The silver one.

> *Which one do you want?*
> The crystal one.

> *Which vases come from Taiwan?*
> The ceramic ones.

> *Which ones come from Czechoslovakia?*
> The crystal ones.

c)   **What** asks a more general question. It can be used with or without a noun.

> *What radio program do you enjoy?*
> The news.

__What__ does Salvatore listen to?
Rock music.

3.5 ADJECTIVES OF QUANTITY

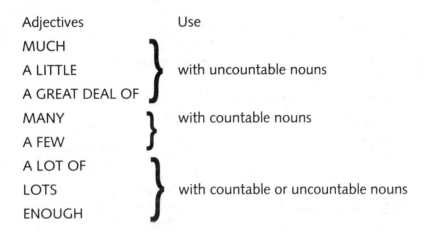

Adjectives	Use
MUCH	
A LITTLE	} with uncountable nouns
A GREAT DEAL OF	
MANY	} with countable nouns
A FEW	
A LOT OF	
LOTS	} with countable or uncountable nouns
ENOUGH	

MUCH, MANY

Much and **many** mean indefinite quantities. *Much* is used before uncountable nouns and *many* is used before countable nouns.
Much is not often used in affirmative sentences. **A lot of** or **lots of** is used instead.
>*He doesn't have **much** patience, but he has **a lot of** courage.*
>*Do you have **many** English books?*

A FEW, A LITTLE

A few means a small number and is used before countable nouns.
A little means a small quantity and is used before uncountable nouns.
>*I need **a few** books from the library.*
>*She has **a little** money in the bank.*

Little and *few* without the article *a* express lack and have almost a negative meaning.
>*They have **little** food.*
>*We have **few** friends.*

> **A great deal of** means a large quantity. It is used with uncountable nouns only.
>
> > *She has **a great deal of** patience.*
> > *He doesn't have **a great deal** of money.*

> **A lot of** and **lots of** refer to a large quantity.
> > *We eat **a lot**.*
> > *They had **lots of** toys.*
> > *Do you read **a lot of** English books?*
> > *She doesn't meet **a lot of** people.*

> **Enough** means sufficient.
> > *Do you have **enough** bread for dinner?*
> > *Yes, I do.*
> > *He doesn't have **enough** money for lunch.*

3.6 INFORMATION QUESTIONS WITH *HOW MUCH* AND *HOW MANY*

How much asks the quantity of an uncountable noun. **How many** asks the quantity of a countable noun. Both can be used with or without a noun.

> *How much chalk do you need?*
> *A boxful.*
> *How much does Linda need?*
> *Two pieces.*
>
> *How many students go home for lunch?*
> *Ten.*
> *How many eat at school?*
> *Fifteen.*

A few, a little, enough, more, less, much or **many** can be used without the noun, if the noun is understood.

Do you have any stamps?
*Yes, I have **a few**. (stamps)*

Do you speak English?
*Yes, **a little**. (English)*

I don't have enough paint.
*I need **more**. (paint)*

*He likes good food but he doesn't eat **much**. (food)*

3.7 SOME EXPRESSIONS OF QUANTITY, MEASURE, UNIT

a bar of candy, soap
a blade of grass
a cup of sugar, tea, coffee
a drop of oil, rain, water
an ear of corn
a handful of sand
a slice of meat, pizza
a bottle of wine, beer
a bunch of flowers
a book of matches
a spoonful of sugar
a pinch of salt
a glass of milk
a pile of clothes
a drawerful of socks
a sheet of paper
a stick of chalk
a ball of yarn/string

a can of tuna, peas
a head of lettuce, cabbage
a loaf of bread
a lump of sugar
a piece of bread, cake, pie
a scoop of ice cream
a pair of glasses, pants, socks
a pack of cigarettes
a set of dishes
a tube of lipstick/toothpaste
a pile of work/papers
a stack of files
a speck of dust
a layer of cream
a roll of ribbon
a heap of earth
a bucket of water
a bolt of fabric

3.8 EXERCISES

IMPROVE YOUR SPEAKING AND WRITING

1. Complete the sentences with one or more adjectives from the lists

provided. Use each adjective just once. Add a determiner where necessary. (See 3.1.)

a) *green, offensive, nasty, spotless, weedless, neat, pleasant, rude, kind, courteous, noisy, hurtful, loud, friendly*

The ideal neighbours have a _____ lawn, a _____ _____ yard and a _____ house. They never make a _____ comment or _____ remark. They don't give _____ parties, don't play _____ music and don't have _____ friends. They themselves have _____ personalities.

b) *Italian, soft, fashion, diamond, gold, sparkling, elegant, long, designer, fancy, stylish, leather, fur, extravagant, warm, silk, fast, colourful, sports, cheerful, gourmet, French*

The _____ actress buys many _____ gowns. She wears _____ rings, _____ bracelets, _____ earrings and _____ necklaces. She collects _____ shoes, _____ handbags, _____ coats and _____ sportscars; she has three _____ cats and six _____ dogs. She knows many _____ boutiques and a lot of _____ restaurants.

c) *old, quiet, romantic, cozy, young, little, large, beautiful, colourful, tall, mature, glass, wide, patio, deep, fresh*

My friend Mario loves his _____ apartment. He enjoys the _____ building and _____ neighbourhood. In the morning, he opens the _____ door and takes a _____ breath of _____ air. He admires the view: the _____ trees, the _____ bushes, the _____ flowers and the _____ street beyond.

d)   *heavy, rich, skinless, creamy, plain, light, fried, lean, low-calorie, red, sweet, alcoholic, green, low-fat, skim, clear*

My doctor told me: "From now on, no more _____ desserts and _____ sauces. Choose _____ meat and preferably _____ chicken. Avoid _____ foods and _____ drinks. Have a lot of _____ water and drink only _____ milk. Have three servings of _____ vegetables a day. Finally, remember: no _____ cakes or ice cream! Have three _____ meals a day."

2.   Work with a partner. You and your partner will create questions for the following answers.

EXAMPLE: Hot chocolate. **What do you drink in the morning?**

a) _____   A movie ticket.

b) _____   The red one.

c) _____   An apple orchard.

d) _____   Race horses.

e) _____   Twenty-five dollars.

f) _____   Asparagus and bean sprouts.

g) _____   Old cars.

h) _____   The Italian magazine.

i) _____   The mail.

j) _____   The tall black woman.

k) _____   Volleyball.

l) _____   Hot and spicy.

3.   The following are short dialogues between Anita and Bernie. Work with a partner, each of you taking on one of the parts.

Complete the dialogues with appropriate words or expressions.
Use adjectives when possible.

EXAMPLE: Anita: What kind of movies do you enjoy?

Bernie: Love stories.

Anita: How many movies a week do you watch?

Bernie: About four.

a)   A: _____ ?

B: Five cups a day.

A: What kind of coffee do you drink?

B: _____ .

b)   A: _____ room needs painting?

B: The family room.

A: _____ one needs wallpapering?

B: _____ .

c)   A: _____ ?

B: I watch science documentaries, soap operas and the news.

A: _____ ?

B: Yes, I watch the 11 o'clock news.

d)   A: What kind of pizza would you like?

B: _____ .

A: _____ slices do you need?

B: _____ .

e)   A: _____ do the _____ bracelets cost?

B: Which ones? The yellow or white gold ones?

A: _____ .

B: They cost $300 each.

f)   A: _____ do you need?

B: A warm winter coat.

A: _____ do you prefer?

B: Brown, beige or cream.

g)   A: What kind of food do you like?

      B: _____ .

      A: What _____ restaurants do you prefer?

      B: _____ .

h)   A: What _____ sell?

      B: Clothes.

      A: _____ ?

      B: Oh! All kinds: _____ .

i)   A: What _____ do?

      B: He _____ cars.

      A: Does he also sell used cars?

      B: _____ cars, _____ cars, all sorts of cars and all makes. He also sells _____ vans and trucks.

j)   A: Does Maureen have _____ pets?

      B: Yes, she has _____ dogs and two _____ cats.

      A: Does she _____ in an apartment?

      B: No, she owns a _____ house in the suburbs.

4.   What are these people saying? Follow the example.

EXAMPLE: A: What kind of books do you read?

            B: French poetry books.

a)   A: _____ pen _____ ?

     B: _____

        _____

b)   A: _____ glue _____ ?

     B: _____

        _____

c) A: _____ rice _____ ?

B: _____

_____

d) A: _____ apples _____ ?

B: _____

_____

e) A: _____ paint _____ ?

B: _____

_____

f) A: _____ cereal _____ ?

B: _____

_____

g) A: _____ juice _____ ?

B: _____

_____

h) A: _____ cakes _____ ?

B: _____

_____

i) A: _____ grapes _____ ?

B: _____

_____

j) A: _____ macaroni _____ ?

B: _____

_____

5. Rewrite the following sentences and add adjectives to the italicized nouns. Use the guides provided and place the adjectives in the correct order.

EXAMPLE: Mary, please wash the *skirt*.

(material, kind, colour)

Mary, please wash the long black cotton skirt.

a) The Ramons buy *clothes* for the summer holidays.

(material, quantity, quality)

b) I take *pills* every day.

(number, kind, colour)

c) Don't throw away the *jars*.

(degree of fullness, content, material)

d) Please, open the *box*.

(colour, size, shape)

e) Maya, the *man* wants an appointment.

(age, nationality, height)

f) I remember the *jokes*.

(number, nationality, quality)

g) He wants the *shirt*.

(material, kind, colour)

h) I like *oranges*.

(size, kind, origin)

i) She makes *cookies*.

(size, quantity, kind)

j) Roberto makes *furniture*.

(material, style, quality)

6. Rewrite the following sentences and expand them by adding one or two adjectives to each italicized word.

EXAMPLE: The *tennis champion* coaches *players*.

The famous tennis champion coaches young talented players.

a) The *hotel* serves *breakfasts*.

b) The *managers* hold a *meeting* once a month.

c) The *teacher* collects *coins*.

d) The *designer* makes *gowns*.

e) The *company* needs *representatives*.

f) The *man* prefers a *drink*.

g) The *students* like the *teacher*.

h) The *clerks* sell *appliances*.

7. The following questions are about Aziz, a caterer. Work with a partner. You and your partner will answer the questions in complete sentences using two adjectives. (See 3.3.)

Example: What kind of business does he run?

He runs a well-known catering business.

a) What kind of shops does he own?

b) What kind of parties does he cater?

c) What kind of receptions does he organize?

d) What types of food does he offer?

e) What kind of desserts and cakes does he prepare?

f) What kind of van does he use?

g) What kind of uniform do the waiters and waitresses wear?

h) What kind of service does he offer?

EXPRESS YOURSELF

1. Ask a partner the following questions. Your partner will answer with *little, a little, few, a few, much, many, a lot of, enough,* or *any.* (See 3.5.)

a) Do you have any family photographs at home?

b) How much money do you spend on transportation?

c) How many English-speaking friends do you have?

d) How many French-speaking people do you know?

e) How much do you read every day?

f) How much do you walk every day?

g) How much English do you speak, write and understand?

h) Do you have a lot of free time?

i) How much work do you do at home?

j) Do you have enough pocket money today?

k) Do you have enough money for an expensive dinner tonight?

l) How much sugar do you take in your coffee or tea?

m) Do you use a lot of salt and pepper in your food?

n) Do you use a lot of spices in your cooking?

o) Do you eat fruit every day? How much?

p) Do you play any sports?

q) Do you play any musical instrument?

r) Do you use any cologne or perfume?

s) Do you use any bleach in the wash?

8. Ask a partner the following questions. Your partner will answer in complete statements using one or more adjectives. Then add two questions of your own, and write them down.

a) What kind of sandwiches do you like?

b) What kind of coffee or tea do you drink?

c) What kind of jam do you like?

d) What kind of food do you usually eat?

e) What kind of salad do you like?

f) What kind of salad dressing do you like?

g) Do you like desserts? What kind?

h) What kind of clothes do you usually buy?

i) What kind of clothes do you wear on weekends?

j) What kind of people do you like?

k) What kind of furniture do you like?

l) What kind of life do you live?

9. Ask a partner the following questions. Your partner will answer by specifying size, quantity and measure.

EXAMPLE: How much butter do you buy every week?

I buy one regular 450 gram bar of butter every week.

a) How much milk do you usually drink?

b) How much milk do you usually buy?

c) How much coffee or tea do you usually drink?

d) How much bread do you eat every day?

e) How much bread do you usually buy?

f) Do you buy any ice cream? How much?

g) Do you buy any soft drinks? How much?

h) Do you smoke? If yes, how much?

i) Do you take cream or milk in your coffee? How much?

j) Do you take sugar in your tea or coffee? How much?

k) Do you eat salad? What do you put in your salad?

l) Do you eat pizza? How much pizza do you eat for lunch? For dinner?

10. Work with a partner. Tell each other what you need to do the following:

a) to make your favourite cake

b) to make your favourite sandwich

c) to build a stool

d) to build a kite

e) to sew a simple shirt

Make sure you mention the quantity, measure or unit.

EXAMPLE: To make a delicious apple pie, I need half a kilo of large MacIntosh apples, 300 g (grams) of butter (and so on).

UNIT 4 – THE VERB *BE*

4.1 THE PRESENT AND PAST TENSES OF *BE*

BE IN THE PRESENT

Affirmative	Negative	Interrogative
I am (I'm*)	I am not (I'm not)	Am I?
You are (You're*)	You are not (You aren't) (You're not)	Are you?
She is (She's*)	She is not (She isn't) (She's not)	Is she?
He is (He's*)	He is not (He isn't) (He's not)	Is he?
It is (It's*)	It is not (It isn't) (It's not)	Is it?
We are (We're*)	We are not (We aren't) (We're not)	Are we?
You are (You're*)	You are not (You aren't) (You're not)	Are you?
They are (They're*)	They are not (They aren't) (They're not)	Are they?

Note: The contractions marked by * never appear as the last word of a sentence.

Affirmative	Negative	Interrogative
I was	I was not (I wasn't)	Was I?
You were	You were not (You weren't)	Were you?
She was	She was not (She wasn't)	Was she?
He was	He was not (He wasn't)	Was he?
It was	It was not (It wasn't)	Was it?
We were	We were not (We weren't)	Were we?
You were	You were not (You weren't)	Were you?
They were	They were not (They weren't)	Were they?

4.2   SOME USES OF *BE*

The verb *be* is used to express the following:

- Profession

  Paul is a tailor.

- Nationality

  Is Nick Greek?

- Age

  She is 20. She is 20 years old.

- Size

  The room was large.

- Shape

  The table was round.

- Weight

  The box was three kilos.

- Length

  The river is 50 km long.

- State or condition

  I'm hungry, tired, cold and thirsty.

- Colour

  The dress is blue.

- Price

  Breakfast was $5.00.

Note: When the verb be is followed by more than one adjective, the last two are joined with AND.

*The living room was large **and** bright.*
*The flag was red, white **and** blue.*

4.3 SOME EXPRESSIONS WITH *BE*

It as an impersonal pronoun + *be* can be used to express time, weather, temperature, date and price.

*What time **is it**?*
Let's have lunch.
*No, **it's** too early. I'm not hungry yet.*
***It was** damp. **It wasn't** dry.*
***It is** hot here. **It isn't** cold.*
***It's** Thursday. **It's** January 24.*
*How much **was it**?*
***It was** $3.00 a kilo.*

4.4 TELLING TIME

What time is it? Do you have the right time?

***It's** four o'clock.*
***It's** four.*
***It's** four fifteen.*
***It's** a quarter past four.*
***It's** a quarter after four.*
***It's** four twenty.*
***It's** twenty past four.*
***It's** four thirty.*

It's half past four.
It's four forty-five.
It's a quarter to five.
It's four fifty.
It's ten to five.
It's noon.
It's midnight.

4.5 EXPRESSING DATES

When you are reading aloud or telling someone a date, give the day of the week first, then the month, and then the number of the day. The year is listed last.

It is Thursday, December 17, 1992.

In Canada, abbreviated dates are written day, month, year.

April 1, 1992 / 1-4-92 / 1/4/92

4.6 INFORMATION QUESTIONS WITH *HOW* + ADJECTIVE + *BE*

The phrase *how* + Adjective + *be* is used to ask about age, height, distance, width, weight, size or condition.

How old is *the Opera House?*
How tall is *it?*
How wide is *the stage?*
How heavy are *the crystal chandeliers?*
How large are *the dressing rooms?*
How modern is *the heating system?*

4.7 QUESTIONS WITH *WHAT* AND *WHO* + *BE*

What asks about a thing or an animal.

What is it?
It's a garlic press.
It's a groundhog.

Who asks the name of a person or the relationship.
> *Who is he?*
> *He's Mr. Chan. He's my boss.*

Note: In a question with *who* or *what* + *be*, the verb *be* agrees with the noun that follows it.

Who is *that boy?*	**Who are** *those boys?*
Who is *Mr. Lee?*	**Who are** *Mr. Lee and Mr. Chan?*
What is *this thing?*	**What are** *these things?*
What is *it?*	**What are** *they?*

4.8 LINKING VERBS

The verb *be* has little meaning by itself. It is a link between the subject and the complement of the sentence. It is called a **linking verb**.

Linking verbs are usually followed by adjectives that modify or describe the subject. The most common linking verbs are *be, appear, feel, look, seem, smell, sound, taste* and *become*.
> *George **feels** sick.*
> *The children **look** tired.*
> *They **seem** confused.*
> *The jam **tastes** sour.*

4.9 *THERE IS/THERE ARE*

There is and *there are* are introductory phrases that show the existence of something. The verb *be* agrees in number with the subject that follows the phrase.
> *There **is** a cheque book on the desk.*
> *There **was** a lamp on the table.*
> *There **are** some application forms in the drawer.*
> *There **were** five students in the lab.*

In everyday conversation, the contractions *there isn't, there aren't, there wasn't* and *there weren't* are used.
> *There **isn't** enough sugar for our coffee.*
> *There **weren't** many people in the supermarket this morning.*

4.10 *HERE IS/THERE IS*

Here and **there** can be used as the subject of **be** to tell the location of someone or something. *Here* refers to an object near the speaker. *There* refers to an object away from the speaker.

> **Here is** *Afna!*
> **There is** *the missing book!*
> **Here are** *the reports that you want.*

Note: *It is*, in contrast, is used to indicate time, distance, weather. (See 4.3, 4.4, 4.5.)

> **It is** *ten o'clock.*
> **It is** *cold today.*

4.11 EXERCISES

PRACTICE YOUR PRONUNCIATION

1. Pronounce *is* as /z/ in the following sentences:

Carl is in the office.	Peter is 20 years old.
The supervisor is away today.	The vacuum cleaner is heavy.
Marina is very busy today.	Salma is in a meeting.

2. Pronounce *is* as /Iz/ in the following sentences. Note the position of *is* in each sentence.

Yes, it is.	Here it is.	Is it expensive?
Wolf is.	There she is.	Of course, it is.
Is it ready?	Is he there?	Yes, she is.

3. Pronounce *isn't* as /IzInt/ in the following sentences:

Marcia isn't here.	It isn't possible.	Rosa isn't Greek.
Gilles isn't tall.	She isn't Polish.	The table isn't round.

4. Pronounce *are* as /r/ in the following sentences:

The Singhs are here.	The cakes are delicious.
The pies are hot.	The boys are happy.
The cans are open.	The books are dull.
The days are long.	The children are in the park.

5. Pronounce *are* as / r/ in the following sentences. Note the position of *are* in each sentence.

Yes, they are.   Are they busy?

Here they are.   Are they from Japan?

These are.   Are they heavy?

IMPROVE YOUR SPEAKING AND WRITING

1. Complete the following sentences with the correct tense and form of the verb *be*. (See 4.1.)

EXAMPLE: Mickey Mouse _____ real.

Mickey Mouse isn't real.

a)   Céline Dion _____ a Canadian singer.

b)   Alaska _____ a Canadian territory.

c)   Peppers _____ often hot.

d)   Basketball players _____ usually tall.

e)   The computer _____ a great machine.

f)   Athens _____ the capital of Greece.

g)   Washington _____ in Canada.

h)   The United States _____ in North America.

i)   Chile _____ in South America.

j)   The Mississippi and the Hudson _____ rivers.

k)   Catherine the Great _____ American.

l)   Al Capone _____ an infamous gangster.

m)   Bette Davis _____ an American film actress.

n)   The Group of Seven _____ Canadian painters.

2. The following are short dialogues between Ali and Barbara. Work with a partner, each of you taking on one of the parts. Complete the dialogues with appropriate words or expressions.

EXAMPLE: Ali: Are you hungry?

Barbara: No, **I'm not**. Are you?

Ali: No, **I'm not. I'm** a little thirsty.

a) A: _____Are_____ the children sleepy?

B: No, _the children_ . _is the_ mother sleepy?

A: No, _____ . _mother_ just a little tired.

b) A: _____Are_____ you late yesterday?

B: No, _I'm not_ . _Are_ you?

A: No, I _I'm not_ . I _am_ a few minutes early.

c) A: What does Mr. Rogerson do?

B: _He is_ a doctor.

A: _Is_ Mrs. Rogerson a doctor, too?

B: No, she _is_ a physicist.

d) A: _Is_ the new carpet brown?

B: No, _____ . _____ off-white.

e) A: What _____is_____ the chief seaport of Colombia?

B: _____ Cartagena.

f) A: Do you know Carlos?

B: Yes, I do. He _____is_____ a bright young man.

A: _Is he_ Italian?

B: No, _He isn't_ . _He is a_ Spanish.

g) A: What time _by your watch?_

B: _____ nine o'clock.

A: Hurry up. The lottery draw _today_ at 9:15.

h) A: Here _____ Dino and Terry.

B: Who _____ they?

A: _____ the marketing experts.

i) A: Mrs. Su _____is_____ so active!

B: How old _so year_ ?

71

A: _____ 70 years old.

B: It _____ incredible. I _____ impressed!

j)   A: _____ any mosquitoes here?

      B: No, _____ but _____ flies.

3. Work with a partner. Ask your partner the following questions. Your partner will answer adding information when possible. (See 4.2 and 4.9.)

EXAMPLES: Is there any life in the desert?

Yes, there is some.

Is there a blackboard here?

Yes, there are two.

a) Is it 10:00 a.m. now? *yes it is*

b) Is there a radio here? *yes, there is*

c) Are there any windows? *yes, there are*

d) Is it sunny outside? *No, it's not*

e) Is it warm? *No it is not*

f) Are there any clouds? *yes, there are*

g) Is it time for English class? *yes, it is*

h) Are you a student here? *yes, there is*

i) Are you a visitor here? *No, I am not*

j) Is there a teacher in the room? *No, there is not*

k) Is there a calendar here? *No, there is not*

l) Are there any windows? *N*

m) Is there a rug on the floor? *No there is not*

4. Complete the following sentences in your own words.

EXAMPLE: There are many **foreign students** in France.

a) There is a lot of ____*Gold*____ in the world.

b) There are many ____*people*____ in the world.

c) There are few ____*Tigers*____ in the world.

d) There are no _____*life*_____ on the moon.

e) There are no _____*Grass*_____ in the desert.

f) There is a lot of _____*money*_____ in London.

g) There isn't much _____ in Southern Europe.

h) Are there many _____*Hotel*_____ in Central America?

i) Are there any _____ in Japan?

j) Are there many _____*People*_____ in Greece?

5. Here are the ages and professions of 10 people. Work with a partner. Create sentences to describe each one of them.

EXAMPLE: Manfred   25   baker

Manfred is 25 years old.

He is a 25-year-old baker.

	Name	Age	Profession
a)	Jane	28	Journalist
b)	Mario	40	Engineer
c)	Lydia	37	Writer
d)	Lucy	78	Retired teacher
e)	Costa	16	Student
f)	Tom	50	Plumber
g)	Monique	8	Piano student
h)	Nancy	23	Office manager
i)	Fazya	49	Lawyer
j)	John	54	Taxi driver

6. What are these people saying? Follow the example.

EXAMPLE:

A: Do you know Hans?

B: Yes, I do. He is a tall, blond and handsome man.

a) A: _____*Do you know*_____ Nancy?

B: _____*Yes, I do she is shoot slim*_____
_____*charming man.*_____

73

b) A: _Do you know_ Mohammed?
B: _Yes I do He is a kind intelligent serious man._

c) A: _Do you know_ Stan and Lori?
B: _yes I do They are cheerful smiling, funny._

d) A: _Do you know_ Carla and Barbara?
B _yes I do they are loving, compassionate caring_

e) A: _Do you know_ Paul and Lidia?
B _yes I do they are honest, hard working reliable_

f) A: _Do you know_ Su-Ling?
B _yes I do He is a competent confident, ambitious man_

g) A: _Do you know_ Paula?
B _yes I do He is a shy quiet wise man._

h) A: _Do you know_ Giovanni?
B _yes I do he is a cool, calm collected._

i) A: _Do you know_ Pam and Maria?
B _yes I do they are athletic bright, healthy._

74

j)   A: ___Do you know___ Robert?
     B ___Yes I do he is a strong,___
     ___honest, happy man.___

7.   Here are the nationalities and characteristics of eight famous
     people. Work with a partner. Use these nationalities and
     characteristics to create sentences.

EXAMPLE: Marilyn Monroe, movie star, American/famous

           Marilyn Monroe was a famous American movie star.

     a)   Leonardo da Vinci, artist, Italian/versatile/inventive

     b)   Albert Einstein, scientist, German born/ingenious

     c)   Jane Austen, writer, British/influential

     d)   Ludwig van Beethoven, composer, German/brilliant

     e)   Emily Carr, artist, Canadian/extraordinary

     f)   Louis Riel, leader, Métis/passionate

     g)   Elizabeth I, Queen, British/powerful/intelligent

     h)   Mahatma Ghandi, leader, Indian/religious/nationalist

8.   Work with a partner. Create then write questions for the
     following answers. (See 4.6 and 4.7.)

EXAMPLE: **What time is it?**

           It's a quarter past two.

     a)   _____ ?
          It weighs 24 kg.

     b)   _____ ?
          It's two kilometres long.

     c)   _____ ?
          It's three metres deep.

     d)   _____ ?
          It's warm.

e) _____ ?

Yes, there are a lot of South American students.

f) _____ ?

It snows a little.

g) _____ ?

She's the Hong Kong bank manager.

h) _____ ?

Mr. Lang, the new teacher.

i) _____ ?

She's the author of the textbook.

j) _____ ?

No, the wine is dry.

9. The following are short dialogues between Antonia and Ben. Work with a partner. Create the missing questions.

EXAMPLE: Antonia: He's a teacher.

Ben: **What does he teach?**

Antonia: English.

a) A: Peter is very tall.

B: _____ ?

A: About 1.85 m (metres).

b) A: John is a heavy eater.

B: _____ ?

A: He weighs 80 kg.

c) A: The steam machine is very heavy.

B: _____ ?

A: It's a hundred kilos.

d) A: The highway has three lanes now.

B: _____ ?

A: It's 19 m wide.

e) A: *Time* magazine? Here it is.

B: _____ ?

A: It's two dollars and fifty cents.

f) A: Franca? Here she is.

B: _____ ?

A: The vice president.

g) A: The room is large.

B: _____ ?

A: It's 10 m x 15 m.

h) A: The hole is deep.

B: _____ ?

A: Four metres deep.

i) A: Mary likes Maurice.

B: _____ ?

A: He's patient, kind and intelligent.

j) A: I need some mayonnaise.

B: _____ ?

A: One cupful.

k) A: Paul speaks Spanish.

B: _____ ?

A: He's Ecuadorian.

l) A: Josée is a successful businessperson.

B: _____ ?

A: She's 25.

m) A: Alfred is a fast typist.

B: _____ ?

A: One hundred words a minute.

n) A: This dress is quite expensive.

B: _____ ?

A: About $400.

10. Complete the sentences with one of the linking verbs from the list below. (See 4.8.)

feel, turn, seem, get, taste, look, smell

EXAMPLE: What kind of cake is this? It **looks** delicious.

a) Roula is a very active stockbroker but she always _____ calm and collected.

b) Stavros holds two jobs. He always _____ exhausted.

c) Take the coat to the cleaners. It _____ scruffy.

d) Don't buy this fish. It _____ bad.

e) I like this dishwashing liquid. It _____ fresh and lemony.

f) How is Mary?

I don't know but she _____ fine.

g) Children don't like plain aspirin. It _____ bitter.

h) They prefer the fruit-flavoured one. It _____ fruity.

i) Here is the message. It _____ urgent.

j) He's very shy. He _____ red when you speak to him.

k) Somia is moody. She usually _____ quiet and shy.

Sometimes she _____ very talkative.

11. Tell the class about the weather in these places, then write down the information. (See 4.3.)

EXAMPLE: **It's very cold and it snows a lot in Siberia.**

a) _____ in the Sahara desert.

b) _____ in Spain.

c) _____ in India.

d) _____ in Nicaragua.

e) _____ in the Northwest Territories.

f) _____ in the Maritimes.

g) _____ in Hawaii.

h) _____ here.

EXPRESS YOURSELF

1. Ask a partner the following questions. Your partner will answer in complete statements. Then ask three questions of your own, and write them down.

    a) How old are you?

    b) How old were you last year? Five years ago?

    c) When is your birthday?

    d) What's your horoscope sign?

    e) What colour is your hair?

    f) What colour are your eyes?

    g) What's your favourite colour?

    h) What colour is your favourite sweater?

    i) What colour are your favourite shoes?

    j) Was it sunny or cloudy yesterday?

    k) Was it warm or cold a month ago?

2. Tell your partner about the following. Use *there is* or *there are* with an expression of quantity.

EXAMPLE: **On my street, there are many bakeries, two French restaurants and many clothing stores. There are few shoe stores.**

    a) On my street _____

    b) In my city _____

    c) In my country _____

    d) In my school _____

3. a) Bring in a photograph of one or more family members or friends. Describe the person in the photograph to your classmates. Mention some physical traits, age, height and weight, nationality, occupation.

    b) Describe the city, town or village that you come from. Tell something about the size, the houses, the streets and the people.

c) Describe your apartment or your house.

d) Describe your car or bicycle or the city buses. Mention size, colour, efficiency, comfort, price, speed and type of seats.

4. Class Presentation. Look in a magazine or newspaper for the picture of a child, a man and a woman. Study their gestures, clothes and facial expressions. Use your imagination and tell the class about these people.

UNIT 5 – POSSESSIVES AND DEMONSTRATIVES

5.1 FORMS OF POSSESSIVE ADJECTIVES AND POSSESSIVE PRONOUNS

Subject Pronoun	Possessive Adjective (+ Noun)	Possessive Pronoun (Replaces Noun)
I	my	mine
you	your	yours
he	his	his
she	her	hers
it	its	(not used)
we	our	ours
you	your	yours
they	their	theirs

5.2 POSSESSIVE ADJECTIVES

Possessive adjectives come before the noun and agree in gender with the "possessor," the person or thing that possesses. Like all adjectives in English, they remain the same in singular and plural.

> *They buy their meat at Green's.*
> *We invite our parents and our grandmother for dinner every Sunday.*
> *Leo and Jenny are our good friends. Their parents are very good friends of my parents.*
> *Look at this bird! Its wing is broken!*

5.3 POSSESSIVE PRONOUNS

Possessive pronouns are used to avoid repetition of the noun. They replace the possessive Adjective + Noun.

> *They don't like their classroom but they like ours. (our classroom)*

*I pay for **my lunch** and she pays for **hers**. (her lunch)*
***His work** is easy, **hers** isn't. (her work isn't)*
***My children** play hockey. **Theirs** don't. (their children don't)*
***His shoes** were ready, **hers** weren't. (her shoes weren't)*

5.4 NOUNS IN THE POSSESSIVE CASE

THE POSSESSIVE FORM

The possessive form **'s** or **s'** is used when the possessor is a person (or animal).

a)   When the possessor noun ends in any letter except *s*, add an apostrophe with *s* (**'s**).
>   ***Ted's*** *briefcase*
>   *my **niece's** radio*
>   *the **cat's** tail*

b)   When the noun ends in plural *s*, add just an apostrophe (') without *s*.
>   *the **students'** gym*
>   *our **neighbours'** dog*
>   *the **dogs'** trainer*

c)   When a classical name or a singular noun ends in *s*, add an apostrophe (') with or without *s*. In either case, the extra syllable ('s) is pronounced.
>   ***Hercules'** strength/**Hercules's** strength*
>   ***Ross'** timetable/**Ross's** timetable*
>   *His **boss'** secretary/His **boss's** secretary*

d)   When there are two or more joint possessors, only the last one takes the possessive case.
>   *Raoul and **Nadia's** house (the house of Raoul and Nadia)*

e)   When there are two or more separate possessors and entities, each one takes the possessive case.
>   ***Raoul's** and **Nadia's** houses (the house of Raoul and the house of Nadia)*

ADDITIONAL USES OF THE POSSESSIVE FORM

The possessive form **'s** or **s'** is also used in the following cases:

a)   Certain expressions of time

three hour's notice
a day's pay
the year's supplies
a month's work
a two week's holiday
a night's rest

b) Expressions of currency, such as *dollar, mark, pound, franc, penny,* with worth
    *five **dollars' worth** of candy bars*
    *three **pounds' worth** of stamps*
    *four **francs' worth** of ribbon*

c) Nouns or names indicating the house, home or store of a person or a company. The words *house, home* and *store* are understood and therefore can be omitted.
    *He shops at **Woolworth's**. (at Woolworth's store)*
    *They are at their **aunt's**. (at their aunt's house)*

5.5 THE PREPOSITION *OF* FOR POSSESSION

The preposition *of* is used to express possession in the following cases:

a) When the possessor is a thing
    *the leg **of** the table*
    *the roof **of** the house*
    *the bottom **of** the sea*

b) With a possessive pronoun
    *a friend **of mine** (one of my friends)*
    *two neighbours **of ours** (two of our neighbours)*
    *a cousin **of his** (one of his cousins)*

c) When a noun indicating a person is modified by an adjective phrase
    The woman's hat is very becoming.
    *The hat **of the woman at the counter** is very becoming.*
    The gentleman's account is up-to-date.
    *The account **of the gentleman in London** is up-to-date*

5.6 *OWN*

For emphasis, **own** is used as an adjective or noun.
> *The work was my **own**. It was my **own** work.*
> *I use my **own** dictionary.*
> *I never borrow my brother's car. I have my **own**.*

5.7 INFORMATION QUESTIONS WITH *WHOSE*

Whose is the possessive form of *who*. In questions, *whose* is used with the noun to ask about the possessor. It can be used without the noun if the noun is understood.
> *Class!* **Whose** *paper is this? There's no name on it.*
>
> *Raoul! Is this your wallet?*
> *No, it isn't.*
> **Whose** *is it, then?*
>
> *This videotape is not Amira's.*
> *So,* **whose** *is it?*

5.8 DEMONSTRATIVE ADJECTIVES AND PRONOUNS

Location	Singular		Plural	
	Pronoun	Adjective	Pronoun	Adjective
Something near the speaker	THIS	THIS table	THESE	THESE tables
Something away from the speaker	THAT	THAT table	THOSE	THOSE tables

GENERAL CHARACTERISTICS

Demonstrative adjectives and **pronouns** are usually used for pointing out or drawing attention to something or someone. Demonstrative adjectives are the only adjectives that agree with their nouns in number.

This book is Roula's.
This is Roula's book.
*I don't know **these** people.*
***These** are my friends.*
***That** lady over there is Jane.*
***That** is Jane.*
***Those** people over there are my neighbours.*
***Those** are Lina's computer discs.*

That is is often contracted to **that's**. *These are* and *those are* are contracted to **these're** and **those're** in conversation and informal writing.

Who's that?
***That's** our new Member of Parliament.*

Are these seats free?
***These're** free, **those're** reserved.*

DEMONSTRATIVE PRONOUNS

a) *This, that, these* and *those* are pronouns when they refer to something already mentioned or something understood from the context.

*She rents these skates but not **those**.*
*Those books were interesting. **These** aren't.*
*Do you understand **that**?*

b) When *this* and *that* refer to something specific, they are commonly used with the word *one*.

*The blue sweatshirt is mine. **This one** is Paolo's.*
*This student is from Tokyo, **that one** is from Kyoto.*
This pen doesn't work.
*Try **that one**.*
*The black leather wing chair over there is on sale. **This one** isn't.*
However, *these* and *those* can be used without *one*.
*These cups are chipped. **Those** aren't.*
Do you like the salad bowls?
*I like these but I don't like **those**.*

c) *This* and *that* sometimes refer to something general, such as a concept, state or situation.

*She is very bright. I know **that**. (concept)*
*I never go out dressed like **this**. (state)*
Was drinking and driving the cause of the accident?
*Yes, the police suspect **this**. (situation)*

d)   In a question such as, *Who is/was this or that?*, the answer is often formed with *it*, even when people are indicated.

> *What a lovely picture. **Who's this?***
> *It's George, my fiancé.*
> *And **who's that**?*
> *It's his brother-in-law.*

5.9   EXERCISES

IMPROVE YOUR SPEAKING AND WRITING

1.   Complete the following sentences with a possessive adjective. (See 5.2.)

EXAMPLE: I keep **my** money in the bank.

a)   George talks to _____his_____ sister every weekend.

b)   We always have _____our_____ lunch in the school cafeteria.

c)   They do _____their_____ homework right after school.

d)   Luigi and I spend _____our_____ summers in Sicily.

e)   Gina doesn't ride _____her_____ bicycle anymore.

f)   My children don't use _____their_____ old typewriter anymore.

g)   I love _____my_____ new apartment. It's so cozy.

h)   She doesn't like _____her_____ new neighbour. He is too argumentative.

i)   Don't waste _____your_____ time! Hurry up!

j)   Are you neighbours? Yes, _____their_____ house and ours face each other.

k)   You and Fred don't know _____this_____ lesson well.

l)   Finish _____your_____ homework first, then watch T.V.

m)   Mark spends all _____his_____ free time in his workroom.

n) Matilda spends all _____her_____ pocket money on old coins.

o) _____her_____ winter coat is too old! I need a new one.

2. Complete the following sentences with a possessive pronoun.

EXAMPLE: Are your assignments ready?

Gilbert's is. **Mine** isn't yet.

a) My skis are worn out. How are _____your skis_____ , Tara?

b) Where are your bicycles, boys? Kuldip's is in the garage,

_____your_____ is on the driveway.

c) You don't have a dictionary? By all means, use _____dictionary_____.

d) Ray and Corinne don't share their sweaters. What's _____ is

_____ and what's _____ is _____ .

e) Remi? Of course he knows Cynthia. As a matter of fact, he is a very

good friend of _____ .

f) The Mansinhas? Sure, we know them. They are very good friends of

_____ .

g) Omar and Magda tell jokes all the time. _____ are funny but

_____ aren't at all.

h) We have two teenage daughters and our neighbours have two.

_____ go to a regular high school, _____ go to a

private French school.

i) Whose umbrellas are these? This one is _____ and that one

is my sister's.

j) My brother and I have identical roller skates; but _____ are

red and _____ are blue.

k) Don't keep the book if it isn't _____ .

l) Give the ball back to the children.

This ball isn't _____ , it's _____ .

m) The Speranzas phone their relatives in Italy once a year at Christmas.

We phone _____ every month. Our telephone bills are high

but _____ aren't.

n) My sister and I each own a condominium apartment in the same building. _____ is on the second floor (I don't like heights) but _____ is on the sixteenth.

o) Where are your tennis rackets? _____ is in my car and Dennis has _____ .

3. Complete the following sentences using the possessive form ('s, s' or *of*) to link the words in brackets. Add *the* if necessary. (See 5.4 and 5.5.)

EXAMPLE: (roof, garage) _____ needs a lot of repair.

The roof of the garage needs a lot of repair.

a) My landlady requires _____ (notice, a month).

b) I always keep an umbrella in _____ (trunk, car).

c) I post _____ (schedules, doctors) on the bulletin board.

d) Ms. Sanjit is my _____ (husband, boss).

e) _____ (computer, Thomas) needs repairing.

f) Mansur enjoys _____ (classes, Professor Hess).

g) _____ (roof, our house) has a leak.

h) She always attends _____ (annual convention, teachers) in Toronto.

i) I don't need my _____ (financial help, in-laws).

j) We admire the _____ (courage, soldiers).

k) The paragraph is about _____ (life, Pericles).

l) Pedro is his _____ (favourite nephew, aunt).

m) She keeps her documents in her _____ (safe, parents).

n) _____ (name, author) is always on _____ _____ (cover, book).

o) Peter does my _____ (income tax, boss).

p) Please move to _____ (back, bus).

89

4. What are these people saying? Follow the example.

EXAMPLE: A: Is this your sweater?
            B: No, it isn't. It's Mary's.

a) A: _____ coat?
    B: _____

b) A: _____ bag?
    B: _____

c) A: _____ dictionary?
    B: _____

d) A: _____ shoes?
    B: _____

e) A: _____ skates?
    B: _____

f) A: _____ boots?
    B: _____

g) A: _____ cat?

B: _____

h) A: _____ watch?

B: _____

i) A: _____ umbrella?

B: _____

j) A: _____ glasses?

B: _____

5. Create questions that ask for the italicized information.

EXAMPLE: *Katia's* dog is a German pointer.

Whose dog is a German pointer?

a) My *sister-in-law's* piano needs repairing.

b) Our *manager's* exercise routine is excellent.

c) *Pierre Berton's* books are informative.

d) Clara is married to *Emily's* brother.

e) Someone from the cable service checks *my neighbours'* cable systems once a year.

f) The husband *of our Member of Parliament* raises money for the local hospitals.

g) *My students'* compositions are quite interesting.

h) Our mother loves *Madame Jehane Benoit's* recipes.

i) We are grateful for *our friends' help*.

j)   I never remember my *neighbour's* family name.

k)   I appreciate the *Moussas'* dinner invitation.

l)   *My next-door-neighbours'* dog is dangerous.

6.   Complete the following questions with *who, who's* or *whose*. (See 5.7.)

EXAMPLE: **Who's** in the classroom?

a)   ___who___ drives the delivery truck?

b)   ___Whose___ uncle speaks Latvian?

c)   ___Whose___ handwriting is this?

d)   ___who___ doesn't understand the instructions?

e)   ___Who's___ your favourite hockey player?

f)   ___Whose___ pencil is this?

g)   ___Who's___ a good musician here?

h)   ___Who___ plays a musical instrument here?

i)   ___Who's___ Dahliah's brother?

j)   ___Who___ was Terry Fox?

k)   ___Whose___ files do you have?

l)   ___Who___ do these people help?

m)   ___Whose___ boss uses a laptop computer?

n)   ___Whose___ dog barks all night?

o)   ___Who___ plays loud music all night?

p)   ___Who's___ not ready for the test?

q)   ___Whose___ pen is this?

r)   ___Who's___ absent today?

s)   ___Whose___ remarks were these?

t)   ___Whose___ Natalia Galinova?

u)   ___Who___ knows Natalia Galinova?

v)   ___Whose___ novels does the teacher like?

7.   Complete the following sentences with *this, that, these* or *those*. (See 5.8.)

EXAMPLE: **This** book is mine, **that** one is the teacher's.

    a)   _____ pancakes taste delicious.

    b)   I like _____ desk but I don't like _____ one over there.

    c)   Houses are very expensive _____ days.

    d)   Sonia, take _____ dishes to the kitchen.

    e)   Soula, please wash _____ glass for me.

    f)   Look! Isn't _____ Norma's motorcycle?

    g)   Aren't _____ Anita's earrings?

    h)   Please correct _____ exercises! There are too many errors.

    i)   _____ roses look beautiful, but _____ over there look dry.

    j)   Don't use _____ scissors! They're dull!

    k)   Who are _____ people? Are they visitors?

    l)   _____ are the old brochures. _____ are the new ones.

    m)   _____ typewriter here skips the character *s*. _____ one over there needs repairs.

    n)   Please sign your name on _____ line.

    o)   Don't leave _____ plant outside. Bring it in.

8.   Work with a partner, each of you taking a part. Complete the dialogues using *this, that, these* or *those*. Add *one* when necessary.

EXAMPLE: A: **This** coat isn't mine.

    B: Which one is yours?

    A: **That one** over there.

    a)   A: _____ tourists don't understand English!

            B: I can see _____ .

    b)   A: _____ paintings come from an old castle!

            B: How about _____ .

c) A: _____ cards are yours!

B: Are _____ mine, too?

d) A: I have two tickets for a dinner theatre downtown.

B: _____ 's great.

e) A: Are _____ chickens fresh?

B: No, _____ aren't. _____

_____ over there are.

f) A: _____ is Wendy Wood.

B: And who is _____ across the room?

g) A: _____ knife is dull!

B: Try _____ one.

h) A: _____ dress doesn't fit. Please pass me

_____ one.

B: _____ is not your size.

i) A: I don't like _____ style!

B: What about _____ ?

j) A: Both vases are beautiful!

B: Yes, but _____ is crystal and _____

_____ is plain glass.

9. Work with a partner, each of you taking a part. Complete the dialogues with appropriate words or expressions.

EXAMPLE: A: **Whose** car does he drive?

B: **Mine.**

A: Where is **his**?

B: **His** is at the garage.

a) A:_____ wallet is this? Is it _____ ?

B: It isn't _____ . It's _____ .

A: Is he here today?

B: Yes, as a matter of fact, there _____ .

b) A: Is _____ your umbrella?

B: No, _____ .

A: _____, then?

c) A: _____ addresses do you need?

B: Christina's and also _____ .

A: _____ ?

B: Yes, I already have _____ , thank you.

d) A: Do you know _____ woman?

B: No, I don't. _____ she?

A: She is _____ mother.

B: Brenda Hart's or Brenda Donnelly's mother?

e) A: _____ the price of _____ hat?

B: The blue one or the red _____ ?

A: _____ .

B: _____ $50, Miss.

f) A: _____ child is she?

B: _____ . Doesn't she look lovely?

A: She does. I love the colour of _____ .

g) A: John? _____ is Beatrice, an old friend of

_____ .

B: Hello Beatrice. Is _____ first visit here?

A: No, John. Actually, _____ third.

h) A: _____ room is very noisy. How is _____ ?

B: _____ is quiet. It overlooks the back alley.

A: You're lucky! _____ overlooks a very busy street.

B: Mary _____ is also noisy. _____ next

to a jeweler's studio. He pounds and hammers all day.

EXPRESS YOURSELF

1. Ask your partner the following questions. Your partner will answer in complete sentences.

a) What's your first name?

b) What's your middle name?

c) What's your family name?

d) What's your full name?

e) What's your address?

f) What colour are your eyes?

g) What colour is your hair?

h) What's your favourite colour?

i) What's your favourite food?

j) What's your hobby?

k) Who's your favourite movie star?

l) Who's your favourite singer?

m) What's your profession?

n) Do you like your job?

2. Now use the information that you learned in exercise 1 above and tell the class about your partner. Write a description of your partner.

3. Work with a partner. Ask your partner the following questions. Your partner will answer in short statements. If the answer is "No," your partner will add correct information.

Remember to use a pronoun to avoid repeating the noun.

EXAMPLE: Do you use your friend's dictionary?

No, I don't. I use mine.

a) Does your teacher use your dictionary?

b) Do you spend your friends' money?

c) Do your friends spend your money?

d) Does your teacher write in your exercise book?

e) Do your neighbours use your laundry detergent?

f) Do your neighbours answer your phone?

g) Do you pay for your classmates' coffee?

h) Does your girlfriend cut your hair?

i) Does your boyfriend cut your hair?

j) Do you clean your friends' house?

k) Do your friends clean your house?

l) Do you eat your friend's lunch?

m) Does your neighbour get your mail?

n) Do your neighbours barbecue in your backyard?

4. Work with a partner. Ask your partner the following questions. Your partner will answer with a short answer first, then a complete statement.

EXAMPLE: Whose work does a teacher correct?

The students'. A teacher corrects the students' work.

a) Whose mail does a secretary open?

b) Whose passports do immigration officers check?

c) Whose keys does an auto mechanic need?

d) Whose advice do students usually want?

e) Whose advice do you usually take?

f) Whose life does an autobiography tell?

g) Whose suggestions do restaurants or supermarket managers sometimes follow?

h) Whose testimony do the jury and judge hear?

i) Whose birthdays do parents celebrate?

j) Whose pictures do people usually carry in their wallets?

k) Whose pictures do you carry?

l) Whose records do the police keep on file?

m) Whose portrait do people sometimes have in their office?

n) Whose pictures do people sometimes have on their desk?

5. a) Describe your best male friend, and then your best female friend to a partner. Mention hair, eyes, height and age. Then write down the information.

b)   You or a friend of yours has a pet. Describe it to a partner. Then write down the information.

c)   Describe yourself and a female friend to a partner, using the suggested words. Then write down the information.

EXAMPLE: (eyes) **My eyes are brown, hers are blue.**

(hair) _____

(nose) _____

(complexion) _____

(English) _____

(English pronunciation) _____

(dictionary) _____

d)   This time, describe yourself and a male friend, using the same suggested words.

6.   a)   Pick a student in the class. Without mentioning his or her name, ask the class a question or two using *whose*.

EXAMPLE: **Whose** husband used to be a carpet designer? **Whose** mother-in-law is babysitting her children?

The members of the class must give a full answer to each question.

b)   Pick three students and tell the class what you like about each one of them.

EXAMPLE: I like Bernadette's accent.

c)   Pick an object in the classroom and tell the class whose it is and where it is.

EXAMPLE: Aida's purse is under her chair.

UNIT 6 – PREPOSITIONS

6.1 PREPOSITIONS OF TIME, DATE, PLACE, TRAVEL, MOTION

TIME/DATE

AT (WITH THE TIME OF DAY AND SPECIAL EXPRESSIONS)

> *at one o'clock, at 2:30, at night, at noon, at midnight, at breakfast time, at lunchtime, at coffee break.*
> *The baby has a nap at four.*
> *She takes two vitamin pills at coffee break.*
> *We have lunch at noon.*

ON (WITH DATES AND DAYS OF THE WEEK)

> *on Monday, on Tuesday, on April 23, on my birthday*
> *She was born on April 23.*
> *She was born on Tuesday.*
> *We have a meeting on Friday.*

> **Note:** *On* Mondays, *on* Tuesdays, *on* weekdays, *on* weekends indicates that the action occurs every Monday, Tuesday, weekday, weekend.

> *They play tennis on Tuesdays.*
> *We work on weekdays.*
> *They visit friends on weekends.*

IN (WITH MONTHS, YEARS, SEASONS AND SPECIAL EXPRESSIONS)

> *in March, in 1985, in summer, in the morning, in the afternoon, in the evening*
> *They usually leave at eight o'clock in the morning.*
> *He was born in January.*

FROM...TO

> *from Monday to Friday, from nine to five, from April to September*
> *She works five days a week from Tuesday to Saturday.*
> *We go to class from Monday to Friday.*
> *She works from nine to five.*
> *The weather is nice from April to September.*

BETWEEN

between three and four, *between* 1980 and 1990
The baby takes a nap between three and four.
She was a student some time between 1980 and 1990.
The letter B comes between A and C.

FOR (USED WITH A PERIOD OF TIME)

for ten minutes, *for* three hours, *for* several months, *for* a (long/short)
while, *for* a few days/weeks/months/years, *for* the summer, *for* the winter
He needs the car for five weeks.
They usually rent a cottage for the summer.

BY (MEANING "BEFORE AND UP TO A CERTAIN TIME")

by noon, *by* three o'clock, *by* Friday afternoon
Dinner is always ready by six.
I need these reports by three o'clock.

DURING (REFERS TO PERIODS OF TIME WE SPECIFY BY NAME)

during the war, *during* the holidays, *during* the day, *during* the winter
He was in Europe during the war.
She does a lot of skiing during her winter holidays.

BEFORE/AFTER

before dinner, *after* class
We always have some fresh fruit after dinner.
I usually go for a run before breakfast.

PLACE

AT (ANYWHERE IN A PLACE)

at the office, *at* the drugstore, *at* the restaurant
At 10:00 a.m., she was at the office and the children were at school.
Lisa is at the hospital to visit her uncle.

Note: With the words *home*, *school*, and *church*, we do not use the definite article
the.

He was at home all day yesterday.
She was at church last Sunday morning.

AT (COMPLETE ADDRESS)

at 253 Kennedy Street, *at* 101 University Avenue
They live *at* 253 Kennedy Street.
His office is *at* 101 University Avenue.

ON (WITH THE NAME OF A STREET, WHEN THE STREET NUMBER IS NOT INCLUDED)

on Kennedy Street, *on* University Avenue
They live *on* Kennedy Street.
His office is *on* University Avenue.

ON (MEANING "ON TOP OF")

on the table, *on* the floor, *on* the desk
The telephone is *on* the table.
Please put your books *on* the desk.

IN (MEANING "INSIDE")

in Russia, *in* Toronto, *in* the box, *in* the drawer, *in* the classroom
They live *in* China.
He doesn't keep any money *in* the drawer.
The students are *in* the classroom.

IN FRONT OF

in front of the desk, *in front of* the students
The teacher stands *in front of* the students.

BEHIND

behind the desk, *behind* the house
The blackboard is *behind* the teacher's desk.
He has a vegetable garden *behind* the house.

TRAVEL/MOTION

FROM...TO (FROM ONE LOCATION TO ANOTHER)

from Toronto *to* Montreal, *from* here *to* the shopping plaza
They often fly *from* Toronto *to* Montreal.
It is five blocks *from* here *to* the shopping plaza.

BY (METHOD OF TRAVEL)

by bus, *by* streetcar, *by* train, *by* car, *by* plane, *by* ship
*We go to school **by** bus.*
*They never travel **by** plane.*

Exception:
*She goes to work **on foot**.*

INTO (MEANING "FROM OUTSIDE TO INSIDE")

into the room
*At 9:00 a.m., we go **into** the classroom and sit down.*

6.2   VERBS OF MOTION

Verbs of motion are usually followed by the preposition *to* to indicate destination.

The definite article *the* defines the destination (*to the bookstore* – the one on the corner) whereas the indefinite articles *a* and *an* refer to an unspecified destination (*to a bookstore* – we don't know which one). No article is used for an unspecified plural noun.

*We **drive to the office** every morning.*
*They **walk to the park** at lunchtime.*
*He **travels to the cottage** every weekend.*
*Rita **goes to a private school**.*
*Esther and Pierre **go to flea markets** for bargains.*

Note: a) With the words *work*, *bed*, *church*, and *school*, we do not use the definite article *the*.

*Chico doesn't drive **to work**.*
*Armando goes **to bed** early.*
*Pat and Mary walk **to school** every morning.*
*Do you go **to church** on Sundays?*

b) With the names of most cities and countries, except those mentioned in 2.6, we do not use *the*.

*Luis flies **to France** every summer.*
*They never go **to New York** in August.*

c) Home and downtown do not require *to the*.

*Antonio walks **downtown**.*
*He drives **home** after work.*

6.3 PREPOSITIONS IN QUESTIONS

Prepositions can come at the end of questions, if the preposition can be used in the answer.

*What does he write **on**?*
(On) the blackboard.

*Who do they usually talk **to**?*
(To) their friends.

*Where do they come **from**?*
(From) Japan.

*Where does she fly **to**?*
(To) New York.

*Who do they always listen **to**?*
(To) the teacher.

6.4 INFORMATION QUESTIONS WITH *WHEN* AND *WHERE*

When asks for the time of an action or situation. **Where** asks for the place of an action or situation. Both are used with the interrogative form of the verb.

When *do you go shopping?*
On Friday evenings.
Where *do you go shopping?*
Downtown.

6.5 PLACE AND TIME EXPRESSIONS IN A SENTENCE

Note the word order in the following sentence:

Subject + verb + object + place expression + time expression
We   play volleyball   in the park   on Saturday mornings.

For emphasis or variety, we can put the time expression at the beginning of the sentence.

On Saturday mornings, we play volleyball in the park.

6.6   ADJECTIVE PHRASES INTRODUCED BY PREPOSITIONS

An **adjective phrase** is a group of words without a verb that has the same function as an adjective. It can be introduced by a preposition and it follows the noun it describes.

*the girl **in the blue dress***
*documentaries **on different cultures***

In the blue dress and *on different cultures* are adjective phrases because they do the work of adjectives. *In the blue dress* describes the girl, and *on different cultures* describes the documentaries.

*The girl **in the blue dress** plays the guitar.*
*He produces documentaries **on different cultures**.*

6.7   OBJECT PRONOUNS

Subject	Object
I	me
you	you
he	him
she	her
it	it
we	us
you	you
they	them

When the object of a verb or a preposition is a pronoun, the object form of the pronoun is used.

*Sally knows **me**.*
*She knows **you**.*
*She knows **Raja**./She knows **him**.*
*She knows **Ruth**./She knows **her**.*
*She knows **the lesson**./She knows **it**.*
*She knows **Tim** and **me**./She knows **us**.*
*She knows **Tim** and **Milan**./She knows **them**.*
*We listen to **the radio**./We listen to **it**.*
*We listen to **our parents**./We listen to **them**.*
*We listen to **our teacher**./We listen to **him/her**.*

6.8   TWO-WORD VERBS

A Verb + Preposition combination usually alters the meaning of the verb itself. We will call these combinations **two-word verbs**. Two-word verbs (sometimes they are actually three-word verbs) are usually idioms.

Learn the following idioms.

call up	*I visit my parents once a week but I **call** them **up** every second day.*
fill in/fill out	*We **fill in/out** an application form for a job.*
get in	*We **get in** a car.*
get off	*We **get off** a bus/train/plane.*
get on	*We **get on** a bus/train/plane.*
get out of	*We **get out of** a car/room/building.*
get to	*We **get to** school at about 8:30 a.m.*
get up	*I **get up** at six o'clock every morning.*
lie down	*When I need a rest, I **lie down**.*
listen to	*I **listen to** the news on the radio every morning.*
look at	*When someone talks to us, we **look at** them.*
look for	*When we lose something, we **look for** it.*
look up	*I always **look up** difficult words in my dictionary.*
pay attention to	*Pay **attention to** the teacher! Stop talking!*

put on	In winter, before I leave my house, I **put on** a warm coat and warm boots.
take off	When I get home, I **take off** my coat and boots.
put down	Stop writing now. **Put** your pen **down** and listen to the teacher.
put up	Teenagers **put up** pictures of their favourite singers and actors on their bedroom walls.
stand up	In the army, soldiers **stand up** for inspection.
turn on	When it gets dark in the room, we **turn on** the lights.
turn off	Before we go to bed, we **turn off** the lights.

6.9 EXERCISES

IMPROVE YOUR SPEAKING AND WRITING

1. Complete the following sentences with *in*, *on* or *at* where necessary. (See 6.1.)

Orlando has some orange juice __in__ the morning, a cup of tea __at__ noon and a glass of milk __at__ night. He doesn't eat much __in__ the morning, just a piece of toast with butter and jam. He has some fruit __at__ lunchtime and some meat and vegetables __in__ the evening.

He works from nine __in__ the morning to five __in__ the afternoon. He takes two coffee breaks, one __in__ the morning and one __in__ the afternoon.

He works five days a week. __on__ Saturday morning, he plays football; __in__ the afternoon, he goes grocery shopping, and __in__ the evening, he goes dancing. __on__ Sundays, he stays __at__ home and takes it easy.

He takes two vacations a year, one __in__ the summer and one __in__ the winter.

2. What are these people saying? Follow the example.

EXAMPLE:

A: Where is the chicken?
B: It's in the cat's mouth.

a) A: _____ the pants?
   B: _____

b) A: _____ the flower?
   B: _____

c) A: _____ Kelly?
   B: _____

d) A: _____ Nadia?
   B: _____

e) A: _____ Jerry?
   B: _____

f) A: _____ the dog?
   B: _____

g) A: _____ Coco's address?

B: _____

h) A: _____ the film?

B: _____

3. Work with a partner. Complete the following sentences in your own words. Follow the style of exercise 1 above.

I _____ morning, a _____ noon and

_____ night. I _____ morning, I

_____ lunchtime and _____ evening.

I begin _____ and finish _____ . I

_____ one _____ . I

_____ week. On Saturday mornings _____ ;

_____ afternoon,

I _____ and _____

_____ . On Sundays,

_____ .

I take _____ .

4. Work with a partner. Complete the following sentences in your own words. Follow the style of exercises 1 and 3 above.

a) Georgette leaves home at _____ and gets

_____ at _____

_____ . She lives in

_____ at _____

_____ . Her parents live on

_____ in _____ .

b) Georgette works for _____ .
She doesn't have a telephone at _____ . She uses the
public telephone in _____ during
_____ . Georgette's two daughters study
commercial art at _____ . Her son is a
lab technician with _____ .

c) Fernando and Anna come from _____ . They both
teach pharmacology at _____ in _____ .
Their son, Carlos, is a professional singer. He is a member of _____
_____ . He sings in _____ .
He also sings at _____ on _____ .
Their daughter, Eugenia, works with _____ in
_____ . She works four days a week
from _____ to _____ , _____
_____ to _____ .

d) My neighbours, the MacLeans, manage a meat shop. They leave their
house well before _____ in _____
_____ and don't get back before _____ in
_____ . They usually drive to _____ .
Their shop is on _____ between _____
and _____ , right in front of _____ .
They park their car _____ behind _____ .

5. Complete the following sentences with a preposition where
necessary.
a) Our son's university is _____to_____ two hours' drive _____from_____ our house.
b) My Korean friend receives a letter _____from_____ her boyfriend _____in_____
Seoul _____at_____ once a week.
c) The painting _____on_____ the wall _____from_____ the stereo is _____in_____ a
famous Canadian artist.

d) Tina was _____ a bicycle accident and she is __at__ home now _____ a broken arm.

e) My brother and his wife always take their children __by__ them when they go _____ holiday.

f) We always have soup __in__ the main dish and dessert _____ our meal.

g) We don't talk __to__ our friends __in__ class time.

h) We sell tickets __before__ the show and sometimes __on__ the day _____ the show.

i) People keep very quiet __for__ a performance.

j) I enjoy politics. I always borrow books __for__ politics __from__ our neighbourhood library.

k) In class, Jerry sits __on__ the back row __between__ Melanie and Raoul.

l) Subadeh also sits __on__ the back __with__ Stephanie.

m) Which airline flies directly __from__ Toronto __to__ Managua?

n) __For__ me, February is a good time __for__ a vacation in Mexico.

o) Be careful! One _____ the legs _____ this table is broken.

p) Some parents save a lot __of__ money __for__ their children's education.

q) Our teacher wants our term paper __to__ next Friday.

r) Why don't you call him tomorrow morning? He's always _____ the plant _____ 9:00 and 12:00 p.m.

s) Stan is _____ a wheelchair. He goes _____ work _____ a special car. He is always early. He is _____ his desk _____ nine o'clock.

t) Maria writes _____ her family _____ Chile every second week. She talks _____ them _____ the phone about once a month.

6. Complete the following sentences with a verb of motion from the list below. Use each verb once and add *to* and/or *the* when necessary. (See 6.2.)

> *go, drive, race, come, fly, fly back, jog, walk, walk back*

a) We usually _____ shopping on Friday evenings. We _____ supermarket but take a taxi back.

b) Renée and her brother like to run. Sometimes they _____ to the park, but then they slowly _____ home.

c) Esther and David like to exercise. Every morning they _____ park and back.

d) My next-door neighbours _____ Europe every summer. They rent a car in Amsterdam and _____ Paris, then Rome. They leave their car in Rome and _____ Canada.

e) My cousins-in-law live in California. They _____ Canada every summer.

7. Complete the following sentences with the appropriate pronoun. (See 6.7.)

a) My neighbours have a beautiful lawn. _____ fertilize four times a year.

b) Zanana has a very good camera but _____ seldom uses _____ .

c) The secretary types all the letters. The supervisor proofreads _____ then signs _____ .

d) Every day, four soldiers peel the potatoes, quarter _____ , then boil _____ .

e) Sima loves hats. _____ buys _____ but never wears _____ .

f) My brother watches "Family Feud" on television. _____ enjoys _____ but _____ don't.

g) Ramon calls Grandpa and Grandma every day. _____ also visits _____ on Sundays.

h)   Our children love wild berries. Every summer, _____ pick
_____ in the woods near our farm.

i)   Yvonne's professor lends _____ his books on tropical birds.
_____ usually asks _____ to return _____ in a few days.

j)   Brenda sees her old boyfriend on the subway every now and then but
_____ seldom talks to _____ .

k)   At the end of their fiscal year, Don and Dinesh write a report.
_____ show _____ to their supervisor, Eva, then
_____ all discuss _____ together.

l)   Fred doesn't like spinach very much but _____ eats _____
anyway.

m)   The company hires summer staff and Mrs. Rehmani gives _____
a crash course. _____ trains _____ , then puts _____
on the job.

n)   Auntie Rosie has beautiful geraniums. _____ grows _____
in her sunroom.

o)   Our Japanese friends invite _____ for dinner quite often.
_____ make _____ a typical Japanese dinner. In return,
_____ invite _____ for a typical Ukrainian meal.

8.   Complete the following sentences with a preposition, where
necessary.

a)   We always have breakfast _____ the kitchen _____ about
7:00 a.m.

b)   Bob and I usually play chess _____ our club _____ Brendon
Street.

c)   Steve is a grade 13 student _____ Brooks Collegiate _____
104 Stamp Street.

d)   The sun rises _____ the east and sets _____ the west.

e)   In Canada, most trees are green _____ summer but lose their
leaves _____ winter.

f)   My supervisor and her family fly _____ Europe every summer. She is _____ Spain and her husband is _____ Germany.

g)   I jog 20 minutes every morning and walk _____ another 20 _____ the evening _____ .

h)   Her teenage son is never _____ home _____ Saturday evenings.

i)   That woman _____ the black suit is our new manager.

j)   Our neighbours _____ usually go _____ work _____ bus.

k)   Every Sunday morning, they drive _____ the country _____ their new silver-grey car.

l)   Salvatore is always _____ his office _____ the morning. _____ the afternoon, he is _____ his trainees _____ the meeting room.

m)   Christians celebrate Christmas _____ December 25th. Boxing Day is the day _____ Christmas.

n)   Many people have a celebration _____ New Year's Eve.

o)   The workers _____ my plant start the machine _____ dawn and stop it _____ sunset.

p)   The workers never smoke _____ the warehouse. Some of them have a cigarette _____ the cafeteria _____ their breaks.

q)   She always practices her guitar _____ two hours _____ the morning and stops _____ lunch.

r)   They eat _____ the cafeteria _____ lunchtime and _____ the restaurant _____ the evening.

9.   Work with a partner, alternating parts. Read the following dialogues. Modify the italicized nouns with an adjective phrase, beginning with the suggested prepositions.

EXAMPLE: A: How much were the *books*?

B: The one (on) **on Eskimo art** was about $20. The other one was $15.

a) A: Who are these *women*?

B: The one (in) _____ is my manager, the one (by)

_____ is my immediate supervisor. I don't know the others.

b) A: Do you know these *people*?

B: A few of them. The couple (by) _____ are my accountant's

parents. The man (in) _____ works with my husband and the

woman (beside) _____ is his wife; the younger couple (with)

_____ are their tenants.

c) A: How much are your *posters*?

B: The one (above) _____ is about $10. The one (between)

_____ is $15. The others are $7 each.

d) A: Who's that *man*?

B: Which one?

The one (with) _____ .

e) A: Which of these *bags* is yours?

B: The one (with) _____ .

f) A: Which *purse* is Clara's?

B: The one (on) _____ .

g) A: What kind of *books* do you read?

B: Novels (on) _____ , books (on) _____ , books

(about) _____ , books (by) _____ . All sorts of books.

h) A: What would you like for your birthday?

B: I'd love a navy blue double-breasted *blazer* (with) _____ .

i) A: Are you ready to order?

B: Yes, please. I'd like a ham and cheese *sandwich* (without)

_____ and a small *salad* (with) _____ .

j) A: Do any of your students speak Urdu?

B: Yes. *The young woman* (with) _____ .

k) A: Which one is your *house*?

B: The small white one (with) _____ .

l)   A: What do you think of their son?

B: Oh! He's a smart *young man* (with) _____ .

m) A: How come you're home today?

B: All *the teachers* (in) _____ are away at a conference.

10. Complete the following sentences with one of the following two-word verbs. Use each verb just once.

put on, go up, go down, pick up, look for, pay attention to, take off, get to, listen to, turn off, lie down, get on, sit down, get off, fill in, fill out, stand up, look up, look at

a) When people apply for a job, they _____ an application form.

b) When the national anthem is played, people _____ .

c) When I come home from work and feel tired, I _____ for a few minutes.

d) Please _____ the lights before you leave the _____ office.

e) We always _____ the news on the radio in the morning.

f) In class, I always _____ the teacher.

g) I _____ the bus at the stop near my house and _____ right in front of my school.

h) Don't write now. Please _____ and _____ the map on the wall.

i) When I need a telephone number, I _____ it _____ in my telephone book.

j) When students graduate from school or college, they _____ a job.

k) I never use the elevator. I always and _____ down the stairs.

l) Don't leave your sweater on the floor! Please _____ it _____ .

m) I feel cold! Why don't you _____ a sweater?

n) Before we go into the house, we _____ our shoes or boots.

o) I am very punctual. I always _____ school on time.

EXPRESS YOURSELF

1. Ask your partner the following questions. Your partner will answer using prepositions.

    a) What time do you get up in the morning?

    b) Do you use public transit to come to school? If yes, where do you get on and where do you get off?

    c) What do you do when you lose something?

    d) What do you do when you don't know the meaning of a word?

    e) Do you ever take a taxi? When?

    f) What do you do when you need a taxi?

    g) Do you get *on* a taxi or *in* a taxi?

    h) Do you get *out* of a taxi or *off* a taxi?

    i) Do you get *out* of a bus or *off* a bus?

    j) What do you do if you want to talk to a friend?

    k) What do you do before you leave your house?

    l) If it's cold outside, what do you do before you go out?

    m) What do you do with your coat when you get home?

    n) Do you often look at old family photographs?

    o) When the teacher explains something, what do you do?

    p) Do you listen to your teacher? Your friends?

    q) What do you do when you are tired?

    r) Do you walk out of a movie theatre when you don't like the movie, or do you stay till the end?

    s) Do you get on a crowded bus or wait for the next one?

    t) What do you do when you see a pen on the floor?

    u) When it's dark in the room, what do you do?

v)   What do you do before you go to bed?

w)   What are three things in your house that you turn on or off?

x)   When do people fill in application forms?

2.   **Work with a partner. Together, create sentences for both (a) and (b). Then write the sentences down.**

a)   Tell your partner where and how often you drive, walk, jog, run, swim (mention where to).

b)   Tell your partner where you go every day, once a week, occasionally, once in a while, never.

3.   **Tell the class which of the following activities you do. When do you do these activities? How often? Make sentences with *go*.**

dancing, swimming, shopping, skiing, skating, fishing

EXAMPLE: I **go dancing** once a week, usually on Saturday nights.

4.   **Ask your partner the following questions. Your partner will answer. Then add a few questions of your own. Write down the answers to the questions.**

a)   What day were you born on? What time?

b)   Where were you born? Where do you come from?

c)   Where do you live? (city/country/full address)

d)   Do you have a job? If yes, what is it?

e)   How do you go to school? To work?

f)   What time do you usually go to bed?

g)   What time do you have lunch? Dinner?

h)   Where do you have lunch? Dinner?

i)   Do you watch the news? Where? When?

j)   Do you watch movies? Where? When?

k)   Do you read books? Where do you get them?

l)   Where do you shop for clothes?

m)   Where do you do your grocery shopping?

n)   Where do you keep your savings?

o) Where do you keep your family photographs?

p) Where do you keep your telephone directory?

q) Where do you go on Saturdays? On Sundays?

r) When do you usually study?

5. Ask your partner the following questions. Your partner will answer. Then add a few questions of your own.

a) Where do students sit and work in the classroom?

b) Where do you sit in the classroom?

c) Who sits in front of you? Who sits behind you?

d) Where does the teacher stand?

e) Where do students go at lunchtime?

f) Where do you go?

g) When do students socialize with their classmates?

h) When do students make phone calls at school?

i) Where do students go for advice and guidance?

j) Where do people learn a trade or a profession?

k) How do we go from one part of the city to another?

l) How do people travel to distant places?

m) Do we, in this country, drive on the right or left side of the road?

n) On which side of the road do people in England drive?

o) When is the summer season in this part of the world?

p) When is the winter season?

q) When does spring arrive?

r) When does it get dark?

6. Ask your partner the following questions. Your partner will answer in complete statements using pronouns where possible.

a) How often do you visit your friends?

b) How often do you talk to your friends on the phone?

c) How often do you go out with your best friend?

d) How often do you use your dictionary?

e) How many exercises does the teacher give you every day?

f) Does your teacher give you any homework?

g) Where do you write your assignments?

h) How many classes a day does your teacher teach you?

i) Does the teacher ask you any questions?

j) When and where do people wear heavy boots?

k) When and where do you wear your shorts?

l) How often do you see your dentist?

m) Do you ever borrow something from your next-door neighbour?

n) Does your next-door neighbour ever invite you over for coffee?

7. Read each of the following items and tell your partner where it is or where you keep it in your home. Be as specific as you can.

EXAMPLE: sneakers

My sneakers are on the bottom shelf in the hall closet.

a) your house keys

b) salt and pepper

c) your telephone book

d) your toothbrush and toothpaste

e) your passport and various documents

f) your radio

g) your favourite picture

h) your laundry detergent

UNIT 7 – THE SIMPLE PAST TENSE

7.1 PAST FORMS OF REGULAR VERBS

The past tense of regular verbs is formed by adding *d* to the simple form of verbs ending in *e*, and *ed* to all others.

I	LIVE	in an apartment.
I	LIVED	in a house last year.
He	SMOKES	cigarettes.
He	SMOKED	a pipe last night.
He	WALKS	to work.
He	WALKED	to work yesterday.

SPELLING VARIATIONS

a)   When the verb ends in a consonant + *y*, change *y* to *ied*.

I	STUDY	English.
He	STUDIED	English.
We	WORRY	before exams.
We	WORRIED	before exams.

Exception: We **play** cards.   We **played** cards.

b)   When the verb ends in a vowel + a single consonant, double the consonant and add *ed*.

We	STOP	at a red light.
We	STOPPED	at a red light.
I	SHOP	on Fridays.
I	SHOPPED	on Fridays.

c) When the final syllable of the verb ending in a consonant is unstressed, add *ed*.

We	LISTEN	to the teacher.
We	LISTENED	to the teacher.
They	VISIT	their aunt.
They	VISITED	their aunt.
He	SUFFERS	from arthritis.
He	SUFFERED	from arthritis.

7.2 PAST FORMS OF IRREGULAR VERBS

About 140 English verbs do not form their past tense by adding *d* or *ed*. These irregular verbs form their past tense in special ways. You must memorize their simple and past forms. See section 7.11 for a list of the most common irregular verbs.

7.3 THE INTERROGATIVE FORM

The past form of the auxiliary *do* is **did**. Like *do*, *did* is also used to ask questions – questions about the past. *Did* does not change in the third person singular and the verb is always in the infinitive form.

	DID	you	STUDY	the lesson?
How many shirts	DID	Ron	BUY	yesterday?
Where	DID	John and Tamsin	GO	on Saturday night?
When	DID	you	SEE	Nancy?

7.4 THE NEGATIVE FORM

Did not (**didn't**) is used to make negative statements about the past. *Didn't* does not change in the third person singular and the verb is always in the infinitive form.

George and Linda	DIDN'T COME	to school yesterday.
Kuldip	DIDN'T WATCH	T.V. last night.
Chantal	DIDN'T PLAY	tennis last Saturday.
We	DIDN'T GO	shopping last week.

7.5 SHORT ANSWERS WITH *DID* AND *DIDN'T*

Did and *didn't* are used in short answers to avoid repetition of the verb.

Question	Short Response		
Did they have a good time?	No,	they	DIDN'T.
Did you go to the tennis tournament?	Yes,	I	DID.
Who invited Sally?		I	DIDN'T!
		John	DID.

7.6 AGO

Ago is used with the past tense of verbs. It means "in the past", and is used in expressions such as these: *a short/long time ago, a little/long while ago, a few minutes/hours/days/weeks/months/years ago.*

> *They began school three weeks **ago**.*
> *I finished the report two hours **ago**.*
> *They bought their house a long time **ago**.*
> *She called the office a little while **ago**.*

7.7 USED TO

Used to expresses a habitual or repeated action in the past. It shows that the habit is no longer continuing or that the information has changed. *Used to* has the same form in all persons and is followed by an infinitive.

She	USED TO	WORK	in a factory.	Now she works in an office.
They	USED TO	GO	to the movies once a week.	Now they go only once a month.
He	USED TO	LIVE	in Ottawa.	Now he lives in Vancouver.
He	USED TO	WORK	on weekends.	He doesn't anymore.

7.8 SOME USES OF THE SIMPLE PAST TENSE

The simple past tense is used to indicate an activity or describe a situation that was completed in the past without any connection to the present. It is frequently used with time words such as *ago, yesterday, yesterday morning, last night, last month, last year, last week.*

> He **finished** his work an hour ago.
> **Did** you **go** to the movies last night?
> They **went** to Spain last month.
> What **did** you **do** on the weekend?
> I stayed home.
> He **wrote** two letters last night.

7.9 REASON/PURPOSE/RESULT

Note: A **clause** is a group of words that includes mainly a verb and its subject.

I left my country three years ago.

This sentence consists of one clause.

She didn't call me because she didn't have my number.

This sentence consists of two clauses:

She didn't call me (1)
because she didn't have my number (2).

REASON

Because and **because of** are used to express the reason why something happened. *Because* introduces a clause. *Because* of generally introduces a noun.

Main clause	Because clause
I stayed home She quit her job	BECAUSE it rained. BECAUSE the working conditions were bad.

Main clause	Because of	Noun
I stayed home She quit her job	BECAUSE OF BECAUSE OF	the rain the working conditions.

PURPOSE

In order to + Infinitive, **to** + Infinitive and **for** + Noun are used to express **purpose**.

*Pedro went to London **in order to** study economics.*
*Pedro went to London **to study** economics.*
*Pedro went to London **for** an economics course.*

RESULT

So is used to introduce a clause of **result**.

Main Sentence	So	Clause of Result
I had a headache	SO	I stayed home.
Few people showed interest	SO	they cancelled the meeting.

7.10 PRONUNCIATION OF THE *D* AND *ED* ENDINGS OF REGULAR VERBS IN THE PAST

The past endings *d* or *ed* are pronounced /Id/, /d/ or /t/, depending on the last sound of the infinitive.

a) Pronounce the ending /Id/ after infinitives ending in /d/ and /t/.

start/start/, started/startId/
visit/vIzIt/, visited/vIzItId/
need/nid/, needed/nidId/

b) Pronounce the ending /d/ after infinitives ending in vowels or voiced consonants.

play/pleI/, played/pleId/
live/lIv/, lived/lIvd/
call/kɔl/, called/kɔld/

c) Pronounce the ending /t/ after infinitives ending in voiceless consonants other than /t/.

cook/kʊk/, cooked/kʊkt/
finish/fInIʃ/, finished/fInIʃt/
like/laIk/, liked/kaIkt/
race/reIs/, raced/reIst/

7.11 PRONUNCIATION OF IRREGULAR VERBS IN THE SIMPLE PAST

The following list gives the pronunciation of the infinitive and the simple past tense forms of common irregular verbs. The verbs are grouped according to the sound changes in the simple past tense.

NO VOWEL OR CONSONANT CHANGE

Infinitive		Simple Past	
bet	/bɛt/	bet	/bɛt/
beat	/bit/	beat	/bit/
bid	/bɪd/	bid	/bɪd/
burst	/bɜst/	burst	/bɜst/
cast	/kæst/	cast	/kæst/
cost	/kɔst/	cost	/kɔst/
cut	/kʌt/	cut	/kʌt/
hit	/hɪt/	hit	/hɪt/
hurt	/hɜt/	hurt	/hɜt/
let	/lɛt/	let	/lɛt/
put	/pʊt/	put	/pʊt/
quit	/kwɪt/	quit	/kwɪt/
set	/sɛt/	set	/sɛt/
shut	/ʃʌt/	shut	/ʃʌt/
split	/splɪt/	split	/splɪt/
spread	/sprɛd/	spread	/sprɛd/
wed	/wɛd/	wed	/wɛd/

/ɪ/ ⟶ /æ/

begin	/bɪgɪn/	began	/bɪgæn/
drink	/drɪŋk/	drank	/dræŋk/
ring	/rɪŋ/	rang	/ræŋ/
shrink	/ʃrɪŋk/	shrank	/ʃræŋk/
sing	/sɪŋ/	sang	/sæŋ/
sink	/sɪŋk/	sank	/sæŋk/
sit	/sɪt/	sat	/sæt/
spit	/spɪt/	spat	/spæt/
spring	/sprɪŋ/	sprang	/spræŋ/
stink	/stɪŋk/	stank	/stæŋk/
swim	/swɪm/	swam	/swæm/

/ɪ/ ⟶ /ʌ/

cling	/klɪŋ/	clung/klʌ /	
dig	/dɪg/	dug	/dʌg/
sling	/slɪŋ/	slung	/slʌŋ/
spin	/spɪn/	spun	/spʌn/
stick	/stɪk/	stuck	/stʌk/
sting	/stɪŋ/	stung	/stʌŋ/
string	/strɪŋ/	strung	/strʌŋ/
swing	/swɪŋ/	swung	/swʌŋ/
wring	/rɪŋ/	wrung	/rʌŋ/

/I/ ——➤ /ɛ/

bleed	/blid/	bled	/blɛd/
breed	/brid/	bred	/brɛd/
feed	/fid/	fed	/fɛd/
flee	/fli/	fled	/flɛd/
lead	/lid/	led	/lɛd/
meet	/mit/	met	/mɛt/
read	/rid/	read	/rɛd/

With the following verbs, the consonant /t/ is also added at the end.

creep	/krip/	crept	/krɛpt/
deal	/dil/	dealt	/dɛlt/
dream	/drim/	dreamt	/drɛmt/
feel	/fil/	felt	/fɛlt/
lean	/lin/	leant	/lɛnt/
leap	/lip/	leapt	/lɛpt/
mean	/min/	meant	/mɛnt/
sleep	/slip/	slept	/slɛpt/
sweep	/swip/	swept	/swɛpt/
weep	/wip/	wept	/wɛpt/

/I/ ——➤ /O/

freeze	/friz/	froze	/froz/
speak	/spik/	spoke	/spok/
steal	/stil/	stole	/stol/
weave	/wiv/	wove	/wov/

/EI/ ⟶ /ʊ/			
shake	/ʃeIk/	shook	/ʃʊk/
take	/teIk/	took	/tʊk/

/EI/ ⟶ /O/			
break	/breIk/	broke	/brok/
wake	/weIk/	woke	/wok/

/ɛ/ ⟶ /ɔ/			
bear	/bɛr/	bore	/bɔr/
forget	/fɔrgɛt/	forgot	/fɔrgɔt/
get	/gɛt/	got	/gɔt/
swear	/swɛr/	swore	/swɔr/
tear	/tɛr/	tore	/tɔr/
wear	/wɛr/	wore	/wɔr/

/ɛL/ ⟶ /OLD/			
sell	/sɛl/	sold	/sold/
tell	/tɛl/	told	/told/

/AI/ ⟶ /I/			
bite	/baIt/	bit	/bIt/
hide	/haId/	hid	/hId/
light	/laIt/	lit	/lIt/

/AI/ ⟶ /O/			
dive	/daIv/	dove	/dov/
drive	/draIv/	drove	/drov/
ride	/raId/	rode	/rod/
rise	/raIz/	rose	/roz/
shine	/ʃaIn/	shone	/ʃon/
stride	/straId/	strode	/strod/
write	/raIt/	wrote	/rot/

/AI/ ⟶ /ɔ/			
buy	/baI/	bought	/bɔt/

130

fight	/faɪt/	fought	/fɔt/

/AIND/ ⟶ /AʊND/

bind	/baɪnd/	bound	/baʊnd/
find	/faɪnd/	found	/faʊnd/
grind	/graɪnd/	ground	/graʊnd/
wind	/waɪnd/	wound	/waʊnd/

/ʌ/ ⟶ /EI/

become	/bɪkʌm/	became	/bɪkeɪm/
come	/kʌm/	came	/keɪm/

/O/ ⟶ /ʊ/
/ɔ/ ⟶ /U/

blow	/blo/	blew	/blu/
grow	/gro/	grew	/gru/
throw	/θro/	threw	/θru/
draw	/drɔ/	drew	/dru/

A FINAL /T/ ADDED

burn	/bɝn/	burnt	/bɝnt/
learn	/lɝn/	learnt	/lɝnt/
spell	/spɛl/	spelt	/spɛlt/
spill	/spɪl/	spilt	/spɪlt/
spoil	/spɔɪl/	spoilt	/spɔɪlt/

FINAL /D/ ⟶ /T/

bend	/bɛnd/	bent	/bɛnt/
build	/bɪld/	built	/bɪlt/
lend	/lɛnd/	lent	/lɛnt/
send	/sɛnd/	sent	/sɛnt/
spend	/spɛnd/	spent	/spɛnt/

NO PATTERN

The following verbs do not fall in any patterns. Pronounce them as indicated.

bring	/brɪŋ/	brought	/brɔt/
catch	/kætʃ/	caught	/kɔt/
choose	/tʃuz/	chose	/tʃoz/
do	/du/	did	/dɪd/
eat	/it/	ate	/eɪt/
fall	/fɔl/	fell	/fɛl/
fly	/flaɪ/	flew	/flu/
forsake	/fɔrseɪk/	forsook	/fɔrsʊk/
give	/gɪv/	gave	/geɪv/
go	/go/	went	/wɛnt/
hang	/hæŋ/	hung	/hʌŋ/
hear	/hir/	heard	/hɜd/
hold	/hold/	held	/hɛld/
know	/no/	knew	/nju/
lie	/laɪ/	lay	/leɪ/
lose	/luz/	lost	/lɔst/
make	/meɪk/	made	/meɪd/
run	/rʌn/	ran	/ræn/
say	/seɪ/	said	/sɛd/
see	/si/	saw	/sɔ/
shoot	/ʃut/	shot	/ʃɔt/
slay	/sleɪ/	slew	/slu/
stand	/stænd/	stood	/stʊd/
strike	/straɪk/	struck	/strʌk/
teach	/titʃ/	taught	/tɔt/
think	/θɪŋk/	thought	/θɔt/
win	/wɪn/	won	/wɔn/

7.12 EXERCISES

PRACTICE YOUR PRONUNCIATION

1. Pronounce /ɪd/ as a separate syllable in the following phrases:
    It accommodated, we visited, they wanted, she decided, you waited,
    they rented, I intended, they wasted, we added, we subtracted, they hated,
    we insisted, I graduated, she repeated, he rested, he decided, they printed,

we shouted, they investigated, they defended, we needed, it ended,
it skidded

2. Pronounce *ed* as /t/ in the following phrases:
    I looked, we reached, they looked, I danced, they picked, she walked,
    I cooked, it kicked, it crossed, she rushed, they parked, I picked,
    they pronounced, you shopped, I washed, they practiced, we laughed,
    it dropped, they developed, we fixed, they golfed, we missed,
    they furnished

3. Pronounce *ed* as /d/ in the following phrases:
    I borrowed, they followed, it continued, they raised, we seemed, I played,
    they leaned, I memorized, it stayed, it opened, it closed, it moved, I ironed,
    we enjoyed, you copied, it travelled, you preferred, you loved, they waved

4. Pronounce and memorize the irregular verbs listed in 7.11.

IMPROVE YOUR SPEAKING AND WRITING

1. Complete the following sentences with a verb from the list below.
    Use each verb once. Add an expression of past time. (See 7.1 and
    7.11.)
    *buy, spend, do, celebrate, have, dry, visit, repair, miss, arrive, bake,
    work, attend, last*

EXAMPLE: He smoked 20 Turkish cigarettes yesterday.

a) Glen _____ overtime _____ .

b) Dimitri _____ his neighbours' broken window

    _____ .

c) Ross _____ a lot of money on summer clothes

    _____ .

d) My friends _____ their parents' 50th wedding anniversary

    _____ .

e) The train _____ at Union Station just _____ .

f) My roommate _____ the laundry _____ .

g) They _____ their wet clothes in the sun

   _____ .

h) Fuad's in-laws _____ a summer cottage

   _____ .

i) The staff meeting _____ two hours _____ .

j) Bernadette's sister _____ a business seminar in the United

   States _____ .

k) Mary _____ many classes _____ .

l) Salvatore _____ a delicious cake _____ .

m) Magda _____ her boyfriend's aunt _____ .

n) I _____ a bad headache _____ .

2. Complete the following sentences with the simple past of a verb
   from the list below. Use each verb once.
   *spend, steal, bite, serve, lose, fall, fight, drive, fly, sing, throw,
   begin, go, die*

   a) My cousin's dog _____ my cat last night.

   b) The actors _____ some love songs at the party last
      Saturday.

   c) My friend's students _____ to the community centre after
      school.

   d) The robber _____ $2,000 from the variety store last week.

   e) My neighbours' little girl _____ her shoe over the fence
      yesterday morning.

   f) Many young people _____ and _____ in
      World War II.

   g) The car thieves _____ the stolen truck 400 km.

   h) The car exhibit _____ just 10 minutes ago.

   i) The travel agent _____ to Cuba three hours ago.

   j) Three-year-old Debbie _____ off the porch this morning.

   k) I _____ all my pocket money on jazz records last week.

l) We _____ our hungry young guests a big and filling dinner.

m) I _____ my ring. I can't find it anywhere.

3. Read each sentence and then create questions with the words provided. (See 7.3.)

EXAMPLE: The Polinski's daughter visited Rome, Venice and Florence.

Who **visited Rome, Venice and Florence**?

Whose **daughter visited Rome, Venice and Florence**?

How many **cities did the Polinski's daughter visit**?

a) Joe bought 12 long-stemmed roses at his friend's flower shop.

Who _____?

What _____?

What kind _____?

Where _____?

b) Marina admired Betty's new oriental carpet.

Who _____?

Whose _____?

Which _____?

c) Miss Yu worked in the reception centre at King College for nine years.

Who _____?

What _____?

Where _____?

How long _____?

d) Wendy's sales representatives went away on business twice this year.

Who _____?

Whose _____?

How often _____?

e) The trip to Ottawa took three hours.

What _____?

Which _____?

How long _____?

f) There were 10 business offices in the building at the corner.

How many _____?

What kind _____?

Where _____?

g) There were many old-fashioned stores between Charles and Leslie Streets.

What kind of _____?

Where _____?

h) The Minister of Culture and Communications announced the opening of the new art gallery at yesterday's press conference.

Who _____?

Which _____?

What _____?

4. What are these people saying? Follow the example. Use a verb in the answer. (See 7.5.)

EXAMPLE: A: Who won the game?

B: The Canadiens did.

a) A: _____ the score?

B: _____

b) A: _____ a goal?

B: _____

c) A: _____ the goalies?

B: _____

d) A: _____ penalties

   for fighting?

   B: _____

e) A: _____ injured?

   B: _____

f) A: _____ the last 15

   minutes?

   B: _____

g) A. _____ the best

   player?

   B: _____

5. Complete the following sentences with the verb provided in the correct tense or form. (See 7.4.)

EXAMPLE: (understand) **Do** you **understand** the lesson?

Yesterday I **didn't** but today I **do**.

a) (go) Sam _____ to France every year but last year he _____ . He _____ to Italy. He _____ alone, he _____ with his friend, Rita.

b) (have) He _____ breakfast at home every morning. This morning, he _____ time. He _____ a muffin at the office at ten o'clock.

c) (come) They _____ for a visit every year. They always

_____ by plane but last year they _____ by train.

d) (visit) We always _____ Auntie Carol on Sundays. This week, we also _____ her on Thursday.

e) (have) He _____ a cold. He _____ a very bad one last month, too. He'd like to see the doctor today but he _____ an appointment.

f) (call) Their grandchildren always _____ them in the evening, but last evening they _____ . They _____ this morning instead.

g) (roast) Every Sunday, the chef _____ a turkey for the hotel guests. Last Sunday, he also _____ a duck and a chicken.

h) (drive) Manuel usually _____ his car to work. Yesterday, he _____ his father's. His was at the garage.

i) (walk) Olivia used to _____ to school. She _____ anymore because she has a bicycle now. But she still _____ to the shopping mall or the swimming pool.

j) (take) Carmen never used to _____ baths. Now she _____ one once or twice a week. A good bath relaxes her. In the morning, she usually _____ a shower.

k) (hear) _____ your colleagues _____ the news? They _____ but I _____ . I _____ our President's report and plans for the future.

l) (forget) Sorry! I _____ your partner's name! _____ you always _____ people's name? No, not always. I remember your partner's first name but I _____ his family name.

6. Complete the following sentences with the verb provided in the simple present or the simple past tense. (See 7.6.)

138

EXAMPLE: Every Saturday, they **go** (go) shopping, but last Saturday they **visited** (visit) their friends in the suburbs.

a) Every year, they _____ (go) to San Francisco by train, but, last year, they _____ (go) to Mexico City.

b) I _____ (know) Tim well. I _____ (meet) him at a party three years ago.

c) She _____ (like) fruit very much. She _____ (have) an apple and two oranges for breakfast this morning.

d) They _____ (understand) the exercise now. The teacher _____ (explain) it to them before break.

e) Raphael _____ (speak) English well. He _____ (study) English at the University of Toronto four years ago.

f) George _____ (not have) any friends here. He _____ (come) to the city only three months ago.

g) They _____ (buy) a farm a little while ago. Now, they _____ (live) on it and raise chickens and pigs.

h) What _____ Joseph _____ (do)? He raises cattle.

i) Kim _____ (import) china from Korea. He _____ (start) the business some time ago, and now he _____ (own) a few stores in the city.

j) What _____ you _____ (do) last night? We _____ (do) anything. We just _____ (study) at home and _____ (watch) T.V.

7. Work with a partner. Discuss the following sentences and then rewrite them using the suggested words with the verb in the correct form. Add your own words when necessary.

EXAMPLE: I entered the room (say good morning to the teacher/take my seat).

I entered the room, said good morning to the teacher and took my seat.

a) He ordered a big dinner (eat/pay the bill/leave).

b)   After Clara and I had lunch, we (clear the table/wash the dishes/go for a walk in the park).

c)   Raphaela sat at the breakfast table (have some toast and coffee with her family/kiss the children/leave for work).

d)   Donald opened the window (make his bed/dust the furniture/ vacuum and clean his room/take a shower/leave for work).

e)   Cindy bought some white paint (remove the old wallpaper/wash the walls/sand them/paint her bedroom).

f)   The cook's helper took some milk out of the fridge (put it in the blender/add some ice cream/whip the mixture/sit on a stool/enjoy his milkshake).

g)   My neighbour dug two big holes (plant the trees/mix some peat moss and fertilizer with some soil/fill up the holes with the mixture/water the soil/take a break under a big mature tree).

h)   First she cut the wood (build the cupboards/put them up/varnish them/then she/sit back and admire them).

8.   Work with a partner. Create sentences in the past with the suggested words. Make any necessary changes or additions.

EXAMPLE: The chair _____ soft/comfortable/she/not buy.

The chair felt soft and comfortable but she didn't buy it.

a)   The exercise _____ long/hard/students/enjoy.

b)   Violets _____ sweet/look pretty/I/not like.

c)   The figs _____ ripe/juicy/taste sweet.

d)   The figure skaters _____ an excellent performance/not win.

e)   The idea _____ original/interesting/not practical.

f)   The films _____ imaginative/informative/not enjoy.

g)   Last week, she _____ ten applicants/not hire.

h)   Last month, he _____ important lawyer/now not remember name.

i)   A few days ago, they _____ cheque/spent all/now broke.

j)   My friend used to _____ landscape/now grow vegetables in backyard.

k)   This morning, the teacher _____ to school/late for class.

l)   They _____ beautiful music/no one dance.

9.   Work with a partner. Complete the following sentences in your own words.

EXAMPLE: Our children came home at noon, ate lunch, then _____ .

Our children came home at noon, ate lunch, then went back to school.

a)   This morning she went to the bank and _____ .

b)   I turned on my T.V. _____ and _____ .

c)   He knocked on the door _____ a few minutes, then

_____ .

d)   Thelma boiled some water and _____ .

e)   They wanted to ski but _____ .

f)   The shoe sales representative got into his car and _____ .

g)   She dropped the glass but _____ .

h)   He washed his favourite sweater in hot water and _____ .

i)   She left the stew on the stove for two hours and it _____ .

j)   The birthday child ate three ice-cream cones _____ .

k)   My partner's little boy had a fever but _____ .

l)   The police officer stopped the driver but _____ .

10. Rewrite each of the following sentences using *used to*. (See 7.7.)

EXAMPLE: People made everything themselves.

People used to make everything themselves.

a)   Long ago, farmers used animals on the farm.

b)   Very few of them had machinery.

c)   Women made bread at home.

d)   They wove cloth for their clothes.

e)   They made their shoes.

f) Families grew all their vegetables.

g) Even children worked the land.

h) They used wood for their fires.

i) They drew water from wells.

j) They made their own candles for light.

11. Complete the following sentences with a clause beginning with *so* or *because*, using the words provided. (See 7.9.)

EXAMPLE: **I didn't buy the coat because it didn't look nice on me.** (look nice)

a) I tried on the sweater but I didn't buy it _____ . (fit)

b) I was really tired _____ . (put on pyjamas, go to bed)

c) It was rather chilly _____ . (put on a sweater)

d) The students had difficulty with the idioms _____ . (teacher, explain)

e) I didn't really want the job _____ . (not fill in application form)

f) He goes swimming every afternoon but yesterday he was sick _____ . (stay in bed)

g) We saw him at work yesterday but didn't talk to him _____ . (be busy)

h) Joe usually goes to work by bus but yesterday he was late _____ . (go by taxi)

i) The company employees got a raise _____ . (go to pub to celebrate)

j) The service at the restaurant was very poor _____ . (leave a tip)

k) The bus was crowded _____ . (wait for the next one)

l) I didn't enjoy the play very much _____ . (acoustics be bad)

m) Every hotel in the city was full _____ . (stay at motel out of town)

n) They had a sale on shirts _____ . (Abdul buy)

o) Miliana had a runny nose _____ . (teacher sent home)

p) I had enough cash on me _____ . (use credit card)

12. Answer the following questions in complete sentences. Use the words provided in a *because, because of, in order to, to* or *for* structure.

EXAMPLE: Why do you go to school? (learn English)

I go to school to learn English.

a) Why was Esther in hospital? (operation)

b) Why did they save their money? (send daughter to university)

c) What did she thank you for? (the flowers)

d) Why didn't you follow her instructions? (understand)

e) Why are the Mansours in town? (visit their children)

f) Why do you walk to work and back? (exercise)

g) Why did you change your mind about a new coat? (need)

h) Why did he leave the classroom? (make a phone call)

i) What do you take these pills for? (headaches)

j) Why were the children home? (storm)

k) What is this truck here for? (pick up old furniture)

l) What is this bakery famous for? (croissants)

m) Why did you turn down the invitation? (have no time on that day)

n) Why did she sell her old sewing machine? (have no use)

o) Why is the teacher upset at Joaquim? (pay attention)

p) Why did René quit his job? (long hours and poor working conditions)

q) What does Jamil need the money for? (a new bicycle)

EXPRESS YOURSELF

1. Ask a partner the following questions. Your partner will give short answers. If the answer is "No," your partner will add correct information. If the answer is "Yes," she or he will add extra information.

EXAMPLE: Did you go to bed early last night?

Yes, I did. I went to bed at eight o'clock.

OR

No, I didn't. I watched the late show.

   a) Did you have breakfast this morning?

   b) Did you have milk with your dinner last night?

   c) Did you stay home Saturday night?

   d) Did you go the movies on Sunday?

   e) Did you go on a trip last weekend?

   f) Did you buy a new shirt last week?

   g) Did you have a holiday last summer?

   h) Did you go to work last week?

   i) Did you write any letters last week?

   j) Did you borrow any books from the library yesterday?

   k) Did you spend a lot of money yesterday?

   l) Did you see a movie last week?

   m) Did you read the newspaper this morning?

   n) Did you listen to the news this morning?

2. A partner will ask you the questions in exercise 1 above. Answer them, then write down the information about yourself.

3. Ask a partner the following questions. Your partner will answer in complete sentences. Then ask a few questions of your own.

   a) Why do some people learn English?

   b) Why do some people learn a second language?

   c) Why do people travel to other countries?

   d) Why do people quit a job?

   e) Why do employees lay off workers?

   f) Why do so many students work in the summer?

   g) Why do people usually save some money?

   h) Why do people usually shop around first before buying something?

   i) Why do we watch television?

j) Why do we watch or listen to the news?

k) Why do so many people jog or go for walks?

l) Why do people go to night school?

4. Tell a partner and then write down what you used to do as a child. Use the following guidelines:

- In the summertime

- In winter

- At night

- During holidays

- On the weekends

- At school

- At home

5. Choose either (a) or (b). Work with a partner first, then write your description down in a paragraph.

a) Describe your last weekend.

OR

b) Describe your last trip.

- Where did you go?

- What places did you visit?

- What did you see?

- What did you enjoy?

- What people did you meet?

6. Work with a partner. Describe a person who influenced you a great deal in your life. What were the qualities of this person? What did this person teach you? How?

7. Work with a partner. Choose an interesting or funny incident that happened to you and that you like talking about. Tell your partner. Then write down the information.

8. Tell a partner what you used to find funny, puzzling, stupid, mysterious or exotic. Why have you changed your mind? Discuss with your partner, then write down the information.

9. Work in pairs. One person is the interviewer, the other is the interviewee. Role play each of the following situations:
   a) A child asking her or his mother where the parents met
   b) An employer asking a job applicant about her or his past work experience
   c) A police officer questioning a witness to a burglary or a car accident

UNIT 8 – INTRODUCTION TO *MAY* AND *CAN* SOME USES OF AUXILIARIES

8.1   *MAY*: PERMISSION

May is used to give, refuse or ask permission. It is used for all persons in the present or future.

Note: *May* does not take an *s* in the third person singular.

*I **may** put off my barbecue.*
*She **may** put off her barbecue.*

AFFIRMATIVE FORM

May is used in the affirmative form to grant permission in the present.

Subject	May	Main Verb
You	MAY	call me at home if necessary.
The twins	MAY	invite 10 friends to their birthday party.
Cédomir	MAY	have a snack before dinner.

NEGATIVE FORM

May is used in the negative form to refuse permission in the present.

Subject	May Not	Main Verb
You	MAY NOT	receive phone calls at work.
The students	MAY NOT	use their dictionaries during exams.
Raoul	MAY NOT	take reference books out of this room.

INTERROGATIVE FORM

May is used in the interrogative form to ask for permission in the present. In questions, *may* is generally used with the first person singular and plural only.

May	Subject	Main Verb
MAY	I	use your phone?
MAY	we	borrow your lawn mower?
MAY	we	give you our final answer tomorrow?

8.2 PERMISSION IN THE PAST

May is not used for permission in the past. For past permission, use *could* instead.

> *For extra exercises, I **could** borrow my teacher's books, but I **couldn't** keep them for more than two days.*
>
> *When you were a teenager, **could** you stay up late on school nights?*

8.3 *CAN*: ABILITY, POSSIBILITY, PERMISSION

Can is used to express **ability**, **possibility** and **permission**.

It is used for all persons in the present or future. The negative is **cannot**, or the contraction **can't** in conversation and informal writing.

Note: *Can* does not take an *s* in the third person singular.

*I **can** help you with the translation.*
*She **can** help you with the translation.*

AFFIRMATIVE FORM

Subject	Can	Main Verb
My sister	CAN	understand some French.
They	CAN	buy these tools at Roger's.
Alex	CAN	play outside after dinner.

NEGATIVE FORM

Subject	Cannot/Can't	Main Verb
Olga	CAN'T	postpone her trip to Ottawa.
I	CAN'T	go dancing tonight.
The janitor	CAN'T	lock these two doors.

INTERROGATIVE FORM

Can/Can't	Subject	Main Verb
CAN	you	translate this for me?
CAN	this woman	show some identification?
CAN	I	leave now, please?
CAN'T	you	change doctors?

Note: In a negative question, *can't* is always used instead of *cannot*.

***Can't** he deliver the order in the morning?*

8.4 ABILITY

Can is used to express ability and skills. It implies the person has the ability or the skills needed to perform a certain physical, mental or intellectual task.

Serge **can use** the electric saw but he **can't cut** this tree down.
*I **can cook** a little but I **can't prepare** a fancy meal.*
***Can** you **speak** Serbian as well as Macedonian?*

The past of *can* is **could** and the past of *can't* is **couldn't**.
*As a child, I **could say** the alphabet backwards.*
*I can speak some English now, but a few months ago I **couldn't say** a word.*

Could you speak some English before you started school?

8.5 PERMISSION

Can, like *may*, is used to ask, give or refuse permission. However, *may* is considered more formal.

> **Can** *I borrow your tool box?*
> *Boris* **can** *store his bike in our garage but he* **can't** *have the key.*
> *Jamie! Do your homework first, then you* **can** *play with your friends.*

Note: *Could* is used to express past permission. It means "was/were allowed to" or "had permission to."

> *As a teenager,* **could** *you wear make-up at school?*
> *That politician was under house arrest so she* **couldn't** *leave her house without police escort.*
> *When she was a teenager, my friend* **could** *go to parties without her brother, but I* **couldn't***.*

8.6 POSSIBILITY, OPPORTUNITY

Can implies that, because of certain existing circumstances, a person has the opportunity to do something.

> *Now that the weather is warm, we* **can** *go swimming.*
> *You* **can't** *swim in the harbour! The water is polluted.*
> *Her new boyfriend is a ski instructor. Now, she* **can** *learn to ski!*
> *We went to Costa Rica on business. Unfortunately, we* **couldn't** *go to the beach as we had a very busy schedule.*

8.7 *COULD YOU*: REQUEST

Could you is used to make a request. It is an alternative to the imperative, and it is a little more polite. The word *please* can be added after *could you* or at the end of the request.

> **Could you** *move this box out of the way, please?*
> **Could you** *please move this box out of the way?*

Note the difference in tone between the following pairs of sentences.

Show me the way to the nearest bus stop, please.
Could you *please show me the way to the nearest bus stop.*

Call me back later, please. I'm busy right now.
Could you *please call me back later. I'm busy right now.*

Please, help me with these boxes.
Could you *please help me with these boxes.*

8.8   *VERY/TOO*

VERY

Very, as an intensifier, increases the value of the adjective or adverb.
*I didn't understand the instructions **very** well.*
*This child is **very** tall for her age.*
*Prague is a **very** beautiful city.*

TOO

Too, as an adverb of degree, modifies an adjective or adverb. It expresses negative excess.
*I can't work in this room! It's **too** hot and stuffy.*
*We can't start planting yet! It is still **too** cold.*
*Go without me. I'm simply **too** tired.*

Note the difference between *very* and *too* in the following pairs of sentences.

*The sweater is **very** expensive, but I still want it.*
*I can't buy this sweater! It's **too** expensive.*

*The food was **very** spicy, just the way I like it.*
*I couldn't eat the food because it was **too** spicy.*

TOO MUCH IN AFFIRMATIVE STATEMENTS

As explained in 3.5, **much**, as a noun modifier, is generally used in interrogative and negative statements. **A lot of** is used in affirmative statements.

*I don't have **much** free time for a hobby.*
*Do you have **much** patience with children?*
*I spent **a lot of** time on my homework last night.*

However, **too much** + Noun can be used in an affirmative statement when the statement implies negative excess.

*You put **too much** pepper on my steak! I can't eat it.*
*Margarita and Oscar spend **too much** money on clothes.*
***Too much** candy is bad for your teeth.*
*My flowers died because I used **too much** fertilizer on them.*

8.9   REVIEW OF AUXILIARIES

Auxiliaries are important in the English language mainly to avoid repetition of the original verb.

DO, DID

Do or **did** are used to form the interrogative and negative forms of a verb in the simple present or simple past.

*How late **do** these musicians work?*
*How much **did** they pay for the violin?*
*She **doesn't** understand the rules of this game.*
*I **didn't** see Mark at the party.*

AUXILIARIES FOR SHORT ANSWERS

Do, **did**, **can** and **may** can be used in short Yes or No answers with the verb omitted.

***Do** you read much?*
*Sure, I **do**.*

***Did** you reserve a table for tonight?*
*No, **I didn't**. I just forgot.*

***Can** your mom take our T.V. antenna down?*
*Sorry, she **can't**. She's afraid of heights, too.*

***May** I smoke here?*
*Sorry, you **may** not.*

***Are** you really **quitting** your job?*
*Certainly I **am**. I have no choice, I'm leaving the country.*

Note: Be as a main verb is also used in short Yes or No answers.

*Were you a member of Amnesty International? No, I **was** not.*

Is she really the best person for the job?
*I think she **is**.*

Is he responsible for paying the taxes?
*He **isn't**. His parents are.*

8.10 AGREEMENTS WITH AUXILIARIES

AGREEMENTS WITH AFFIRMATIVE STATEMENTS

Agreements with affirmative statements are made with **yes**, **sure**, **of course**, **certainly**, and the appropriate affirmative auxiliaries.

*Ingrid Bergman **was** a great movie star.*
*She certainly **was**.*

*Our supervisor **agrees** with our three-year plan.*
*Yes, she **does**.*

*They finally **realized** their mistake.*
*They sure **did**.*

*I see you **recycle** all your old jars and bottles.*
*Of course, we **do**.*

AGREEMENTS WITH NEGATIVE STATEMENTS

Agreements with negative statements are made with **no** and the appropriate negative auxiliary.

*She **didn't pay** for the album.*
*No, she **didn't**.*

*They **aren't coming over** for coffee.*
*No, they **aren't**.*

*Julio **doesn't understand** much English.*
*No, he **doesn't**.*

*Migrant workers **can't work** without a work permit.*
*No, they **can't**.*

DISAGREEMENTS WITH AFFIRMATIVE STATEMENTS

Disagreements with affirmative statements are made with **no, oh no**, and the appropriate negative auxiliary.

*I really **tried** to make a good impression on your father.*
***Oh no**, you **didn't**.*
*You **lied** to me!*
*No, I **didn't**.*
*Johnny, I **love** you!*
*No, you **don't**.*

DISAGREEMENTS WITH NEGATIVE STATEMENTS

Disagreements with negative statements are made with **yes, oh yes**, of **course, sure**, and the appropriate affirmative auxiliary.

*You **didn't do** your homework!*
***Of course**, I **did**.*
*Mom, **I'm not going** to school today!*
***Oh yes**, you **are**.*
*I **can't** eat my vegetables!*
***Sure**, you **can**.*

8.11 TOO/SO, EITHER/NEITHER

Too, so, either and **neither** are used with the appropriate auxiliary in response to a statement made by another person. *Too* and *so* are used with affirmative statements, *either* and *neither* are used with negative statements.

Affirmative Statement	Possible Responses						
He always does his homework.	I	DO	TOO.	or	SO	DO	I.
You talk too much.	You	DO	TOO.	or	SO	DO	you.
Birds make beautiful pets.	Fish	DO	TOO.	or	SO	DO	fish.
Mimi mimics people very well.	Her brother	DOES	TOO.	or	SO	DOES	her brother
We donated some food to the food bank.	We	DID	TOO.	or	SO	DID	we.
My teacher can give me some extra help.	Mine	CAN	TOO.	or	SO	CAN	mine.

Negative Statement	Possible Responses		
I'm not renewing my club membership.	I'm not		EITHER.
We didn't attend the recital.	Our neighbours	DIDN'T	EITHER.
I don't eat shellfish.	We	DON'T	EITHER.
I never drink coffee after 5:00 p.m.	My wife	DOESN'T	EITHER.
My husband didn't request a transfer.	Mine	DIDN'T	EITHER.

Negative Statement	Possible Responses		
I'm not renewing my club membership.	NEITHER	AM	I.
We didn't attend the recital.	NEITHER	DID	our neighbours.
I don't eat shellfish.	NEITHER	DO	we.
I never drink coffee after 5:00 p.m.	NEITHER	DOES	my wife.
My husband didn't request a transfer.	NEITHER	DID	mine.

8.12   TAG QUESTIONS

Tag questions (or endings) are short additions to sentences that invite agreement or confirmation of a fact. Tag questions consist of a pronoun and an auxiliary verb, but not a main verb.

AFFIRMATIVE SENTENCES

An affirmative sentence is followed by an **interrogative negative** tag question.

156

Affirmative Sentence	Tag Question
It's a beautiful day,	ISN'T IT?
Patricia was away yesterday,	WASN'T SHE?
You borrowed my sweater,	DIDN'T YOU?
You're tidying up the room,	AREN'T YOU?
They can mail the parcel,	CAN'T THEY?
The Porrettas entertain lavishly,	DON'T THEY?

NEGATIVE SENTENCES

A negative sentence is followed by an **interrogative affirmative** tag question.

Negative Sentence	Tag Questions
The Dakars aren't Syrian,	ARE THEY?
You didn't hire a lawyer,	DID YOU?
Dr. Trueman doesn't eat oysters,	DOES SHE?
Sylvia couldn't nominate her brother,	COULD SHE?
Susan Lopez isn't running for mayor,	IS SHE?
She never invites her colleagues,	DOES SHE?

MORE NOTES ON TAG QUESTIONS

This or *that* in a statement is replaced by *it* in the tag question.
> **This** *is a fantastic idea,* **isn't it**?
> **That** *was Rita,* **wasn't it**?

These or *those* is replaced by *they.*
> **These** *gems aren't real,* **are they**?
> **Those** *compact discs belonged to Jerry,* **didn't they**?

157

When the personal *I* is in a negative tag question, *am I not* (formal) or *aren't I* (informal) is used.

> *I am my country's representative,* **am I not?**
> *I am entitled to these benefits,* **aren't I?**
> *I am your best friend,* **aren't I?**

8.13 *DO, DOES, DID* FOR EMPHASIS

Do, **does**, **did** + Infinitive are used to add special emphasis, especially when another speaker expresses doubt about the action.

> *You didn't complete the assignment.*
> **I did complete it!**
>
> *She doesn't seem to understand what I'm saying!*
> *Oh, but she* **does understand.**

8.14 EXERCISES

IMPROVE YOUR SPEAKING AND WRITING

1. Give two short responses to each of the following statements, one with *too* and one with *so*. Use the words provided. (See 8.11.)

EXAMPLE: Belgium has two official languages. (Canada)

Canada does too. So does Canada.

a) Polish belongs to the Balto-Slavic family of languages. (Russian)

b) Buffalo is on the Canadian-American border. (Detroit)

c) Nefertiti lived in Ancient Egypt. (Cleopatra)

d) Greece's economy depends largely on tourism. (The Caribbean Islands)

e) Great Britain joined the United States in the Gulf War. (Canada)

f) Los Angeles suffers from water shortage. (the rest of California)

g) The French flag has three colours: blue, white and red. (the Yugoslav flag)

h) The Portuguese speak Portuguese. (Brazilians)

i) Shrimp are shellfish. (scallops)

j) Oranges contain a lot of vitamin C. (kiwis)

k) Dolphins are mammals. (seals)

l) Cigarette smoke can cause cancer. (certain gas vapours)

2. Give two short responses to each of the following statements, one with *either* and one with *neither*.

EXAMPLE: Slovenian was not Yugoslavia's official language. (Macedonian)

Macedonian wasn't either. Neither was Macedonian.

a) The United States doesn't have a second official language. (Mexico)

b) Alcohol can't freeze easily. (oil)

c) Albania doesn't export oil. (Luxemburg)

d) Switzerland didn't fight in the Gulf War. (Belgium)

e) Japan wasn't on the Allies' side in World War II. (Italy)

f) Out-of-season vegetables don't always taste very good. (Out-of-season fruit)

g) Bananas don't grow in cold countries. (dates)

h) Iran doesn't import oil. (Saudi Arabia)

i) A pound isn't equivalent to a dollar. (a German mark)

j) Romanian isn't a Slavic language. (German)

k) Hindus don't celebrate Christmas. (Moslems)

l) Hungary doesn't border on a sea. (Czechoslovakia)

3. Complete the following statements with the proper tag question. (See 8.12.)

EXAMPLE: You like westerns, **don't you**?

a) Your friends have a lot of books, _____ ?

b) You're growing vegetables in your backyard this summer, _____ ?

c) Your parents didn't enjoy my rock music, _____ ?

d) You're inviting us to your wedding, _____ ?

e) You hid the cookies, _____ ?

f) They like this country, _____ ?

g) They argued after we left, _____ ?

h) Tell me the truth! He proposed, _____ ?

i) They are considering our suggestions, _____ ?

j) The Reinharts can't evict their tenants, _____ ?

k) Our new neighbours don't seem too friendly, _____ ?

l) Gladys is a very intelligent woman, _____ ?

m) You want to discuss the offer with your partner first, _____ ?

n) They aren't giving us back the money, _____ ?

o) I can bring up my child alone, _____ ?

p) I'm not getting a raise after all, _____ ?

q) You don't agree with him, _____ ?

r) I am your best friend, _____ ?

s) They can't pay the rent this month, _____ ?

t) These tenants never caused any problems, _____ ?

u) You don't attend any of the meetings anymore, _____ ?

v) This coat is very expensive, _____ ?

w) That tape teaches pronunciation, _____ ?

x) These leaves make good tea, _____ ?

y) Those cookies tasted very fresh, _____ ?

4. A visitor to your school is making the following statements. Express your agreement or disagreement in a sentence using an expression such as *oh yes, oh no, of course, of course not, sure, definitely not,* and an auxiliary construction. Add correct information when possible.

EXAMPLE: You don't pay the teachers for extra help after class.

Of course we don't! It's part of their job.

a) You have an accent! You weren't born in this country.

b) Let me guess! You're from South America.

c) English is not your first language.

d) I don't think you spoke English in your country.

e) You didn't learn English in your country.

f) You can read the newspaper now, can't you?

g) You couldn't read it a few months ago!

h) You don't read the newspaper in class.

i) You don't read foreign magazines in class, do you?

j) I think this is a good course.

k) Students can't really learn to speak well in just a few months.

l) Teachers here use just English in their teaching.

m) They don't use other languages, do they?

n) I'm sure that classes are quite small.

o) I see there are more women teachers than men teachers.

p) I believe listening, speaking, reading and writing are the main skills.

q) You are learning these skills here, aren't you?

r) English is difficult enough! You're not learning another language at the same time.

5. Add a short, personal response to the following statements. You can agree or disagree, as you choose. Use *too* or *so*, *either* or *neither*.

EXAMPLE: We love hockey.

We do too.

OR **So do we.**

OR **We don't.**

They didn't enjoy the play.

I didn't either.

OR **Neither did I.**

OR **I did.**

a) They like country living.

b) We don't like sports.

c) We never go to plays.

d) I don't eat red meat.

e) I'm tired these days.

f) My mother doesn't speak English.

g) My teacher talks a lot!

h) My students need more practice in speaking.

i) We don't make too many spelling mistakes.

j) I can't run too fast.

k) Just a few months ago, José couldn't speak a word of English.

l) We aren't going out tonight.

m) I didn't sleep too well last night.

n) We came by bus today.

6. You may agree or disagree with each of the following statements. Add a short, personal response. (See 8.10.)

EXAMPLE: That's unfair.

Yes, it is.

Oh no, it isn't.

a) You always ask advice from people.

b) You always remember your friends' birthdays.

c) You don't make too many mistakes.

d) Life isn't so difficult after all.

e) Our teachers are the best.

f) They're really doing their best.

g) You don't like animals.

h) I look tired today.

i) My hair is a mess.

j) Our friendship means nothing to you.

k) I'm leaving now.

7. The following are short dialogues between Arturo and Brigitta. Work with a partner, each of you taking on a part. Complete the dialogues with your own words. Use *too* or *very* when possible.

EXAMPLE: Arturo: I enjoyed the picnic.

Brigitta: I **did too**. It **was very** relaxing.

a) A: I didn't like the meal at all!

B: I _____ . It _____ bland.

b) A: You didn't stay till the end.

B: No, _____ . The meeting _____ just

_____ long.

A: Yes, it _____ but it _____

informative.

c) A: You can't call them at this hour!

B: Of course I _____ . It _____

emergency.

A: You call a clogged drain an emergency? They _____

do anything about it now anyway.

d) A: Don't take this road. _____ dangerous.

B: No, _____ . _____ a little bumpy.

A: What do you mean, "a little"? It _____ bumpy.

_____ feel it?

B: It's your fault! You put _____ luggage in the trunk.

You packed _____ much.

A: I _____ pack too much! After all, we're going away

for three months.

B: Honey! You simply _____ clothes. We

_____ need all this!

e) A: You _____ wear these shoes.

B: Why _____ ?

A: The heels are _____ ! They're bad for your back.

B: I _____ the other pair either. They

_____ casual.

f) A: _____ borrow your lawn mower?

B: What's wrong with _____ ?

A: The blades _____ dull.

B: _____ replace them?

A: Sure, _____ . What I really need is a new lawn

mower. This one _____ old, _____

heavy and it consumes _____ gas.

g) A: You didn't call me last night!

B: I _____ call you but your line _____ .

A: Why _____ try again later?

B: I _____ try many times but your line

_____ always busy.

h) A: You don't love me anymore!

B: I _____ love you, believe me I _____ .

A: You _____ spend as _____ time

with me _____ before.

B: I try darling! I _____ try! But I'm simply

_____ with our wedding plans.

i) A: Our new neighbours are very quiet.

B: Sure _____ . But sometimes their son plays his music

a little _____ .

A: Maybe he _____ . I hear he's an opera lover.

B: So _____ parents.

A: I don't like opera.

B: Neither _____ .

A: I prefer musicals.

B: _____ too.

8. Ask for permission in the following situations. (See 8.1 and 8.3.)

EXAMPLE: You want to go home early.

May I go home early?

Can I go home early?

a) You want to close the door.

b) You want to turn the T.V. off.

c) You want to turn on the light.

d) You want to borrow my phone book.

e) You want to check my telephone.

f) You want to call me early in the morning.

g) You want to ask me for a favour.

h) You want to comment on my letter.

i) You want to have my opinion.

j) You want to sit at my table.

k) You want to introduce your friend to me.

l) You want to see my driver's license.

m) You want to borrow my car.

n) You want to use my cottage for a week.

o) You want to borrow lawn chairs.

9. What are these people saying? Follow the example.

EXAMPLE: A: Can you come to my place tonight?

B: Yes, I can.

A: Will you come to my place tonight?

B: Yes, I will.

a) A: _____ use your mother's car?

B: _____

A: _____

B: _____

b) A: _____ arrive at seven o'clock?

B: _____

A: _____

B: _____

c) A: _____ help with the cooking?

B: _____

A: _____

B: _____

d) A: _____ bring a casserole?

B: _____

A: _____

B: _____

e) A: _____ invite Jim?

B: _____

A: _____

B: _____

f) A: _____ watch the hockey
game after dinner?

B: _____

A: _____

B: _____

g) A: _____ go out dancing
after the game?

B: _____

A: _____

B: _____

h) A: _____ take pictures at the party?

    B: _____

    A: _____

    B: _____

10. Reply to the following Yes or No questions with expressions such as *of course, sure, sorry, I'm sorry,* and an auxiliary construction. Add correct information when possible.

EXAMPLE: Can I use the phone in the teacher's room?

I'm sorry, you can't. You can use the public phone in the cafeteria.

a) May I ask you a question?

b) Can students use the photocopier in the director's office?

c) Can they use the staff room on their breaks?

d) Can I sometimes bring my child to class?

e) Is it possible for a good student to skip a grade?

f) Can we always ask the teacher to repeat an explanation?

g) Do students stay in the classroom on their breaks?

h) Does your teacher smoke in the school?

i) Is your teacher teaching you math, too?

j) Is your teacher bilingual?

k) Does your teacher use another language in class besides English?

l) Can I sometimes leave class a little earlier?

m) May I sometimes borrow your dictionary?

n) May I borrow your car?

o) Did you learn English in your country?

p) Did you understand today's lesson very well?

11. Respond to the following situations in the negative with *can, could* and *too.* Use the suggested words, then add your own.

EXAMPLE: Why is the little boy crying with his math book open in front of him? (solve the problems/frustrated/to try again)

He can't solve the problems. He is too frustrated to try again.

a) Why did you cancel my two o'clock appointment with the manager? (see you/busy/to see you)

b) Why doesn't Alina know her piano pieces by heart? (practice/tired/to play)

c) Why is Mrs. Trino calling a taxi? (take the bus/much hurry/to wait at the bus stop)

d) Why didn't you spend the afternoon in the garden? (sit outside for long/cool/to stay out all afternoon)

e) Why are you altering these pants? (wear them/big/to wear)

f) Why are these boxes still on the floor? (lift them/heavy/to move)

g) Why doesn't Raman go fishing with his friends? (take the weekend off/busy/to take time off)

h) Why does Robert take sleeping pills? (sleep/nervous/to relax)

i) Why don't you do Exercise 6? (understand/hard/to do)

j) Why don't you eat your soup? (eat it/hot/to swallow)

k) Why did she send the steak back? (eat it/tough/to chew)

l) Why don't you have a glass of juice? (drink/full/to drink anything)

m) Why didn't the doctor discharge Maria from the hospital last week? (walk without help/weak/to stand by herself)

n) Why didn't you finish your test? (remember the vocabulary/tense/to work quickly)

12. Reinforce the following comments by making statements using *too* + an Adjective. Use the suggested beginnings.

EXAMPLE: Can he stand in line? He looks very tired.

No, he can't. **He looks too tired to stand in line.**

a) Can you carry this suitcase? It is very heavy.

No, I can't. It _____

b) Can he eat? He seems very excited.

No, he can't. He _____

c) Could she go to the movies yesterday? She was very busy.

No, she couldn't. She _____

d) Can Ivana paint the wood? It is very wet.

No, she can't. It's _____

e) Can Mr. Stevens mow the lawn? He is very old.

No, he can't. He _____

f) Can he reach the top shelf? It is very high.

No, he can't. It _____

g) Can he wear the grey boots? They seem very tight.

No, he can't. They _____

h) Can you drink this coffee? It's very bitter.

No, I can't. It _____

i) Can you use this machine? It's very noisy.

No, I can't. It _____

j) Can they swallow these pills? They are very big.

No, they can't. They _____

k) Can 25 people sit in this classroom? It's very small.

No, they can't. It _____

l) Can we have a picnic? It's very cold.

No, we can't. It _____

m) Are Susan's jeans comfortable? They look very tight.

No, they aren't. They _____

n) Can they rent this apartment? It's very far from their work.

No, they can't. It _____

o) Can he take that bus? It's very crowded.

No, he can't. It _____

13. Complete the following sentences with *a lot of, very, too, too much* or *too many*.

EXAMPLE: These shoes are **too** tight. I can't wear them.

a) This apple is _____ sour. I can't eat it.

b) He ate _____ candies. Now he has a stomachache.

c) My grandmother is _____ old but she still drives.

d) Mr. Chiu feels _____ old to drive. He no longer renews his license.

e) This situation is _____ complex. We don't know the answer.

f) Does the cake have _____ nuts in it? Natasha loves nuts.

g) Don't drink _____ coffee. It's not good for you.

h) He had _____ problems. He had a nervous breakdown.

i) Yesterday, Paul was _____ drunk to remember what you were telling him.

j) That community centre is _____ far. We can't get there in 20 minutes.

k) Silvo, you look _____ tense. Relax!

l) Caroline is _____ excited. She is going to the circus this Saturday.

m) Tova didn't talk to _____ guests at the reception.

n) We like this restaurant. There is _____ choice in the menu.

o) She has _____ free time. She is bored.

p) The tornado was _____ strong last night. It uprooted many trees.

q) Why are you standing? There is _____ room in the second row.

r) Grandma's dentures are _____ loose. She can't bite into anything hard.

s) The doctor is keeping her in the hospital overnight. She has _____ injuries.

t) He is _____ easygoing. He never complains about anything.

14. With a partner, read the following pairs of sentences, then make comments using *too much* or *too many*. Then write your statements down.

EXAMPLE: The waitress put a lot of sugar in my coffee. I can't drink it.

The waitress put too much sugar in my coffee.

a) She spent a lot of money on a piano. Now she can't pay her bills.

b) She is wearing a lot of eye make-up. She looks awful.

c) He watches a lot of horror movies. He often has nightmares about them.

d) There were a lot of mosquitoes near the lake. We couldn't go out for a walk last night.

e) She reads a lot. Her eyes need a rest.

f) He made a lot of promises. He can keep only a few of them.

g) They drank a lot of whiskey last weekend. Now they are suffering from hangovers.

h) Ronnie has a lot of paintings. He can't hang them all in his apartment.

i) They placed a lot of long distance calls. Their telephone bill is very high this month.

j) He made a lot of grammar errors. He has to rewrite his composition.

k) There were a lot of weeds at the beach. We couldn't go swimming.

l) He asked a lot of questions. He offended his neighbours.

m) She drank a lot of water. She felt bloated.

n) They planted a lot of vegetables. They can't eat all of them.

o) Spring Building Corporation built a lot of houses. Now they don't have enough buyers.

p) Little Rolo watches a lot of television. He doesn't have time for other activities.

q) She put a lot of rum in the cake. It smells quite strong.

r) They enrolled a lot of students. The classes are very crowded.

s) Don't order a lot of extras for your car. They are not necessary.

t) He has a lot of assignments due on the same date. He worries about them.

15. Complete the following dialogues with *can* or *may*.

EXAMPLE: A: Can I take the company truck tomorrow?

B: No, not tomorrow. We need it. You can have it after tomorrow.

a) A: _____ you use the computer in the next room?

B: No, I _____ . Only secretaries _____ .

b) A: _____ the children stay up late on Saturday night?

B: Yes, they _____ . But they _____ do it on school nights.

c) A: _____ tourists take pictures in this church?

B: No, they _____ . They _____ only photograph the building from the outside.

d) A: _____ high school students smoke on school grounds?

B: No, they _____ . Only the staff _____ and only in a designated area.

e) A: _____ swimmers go into the cafeteria in swimsuits?

B: No, they _____ but they _____ wear shorts.

f) A: _____ zoo visitors feed the animals?

B: No, they _____ . Only zoo attendants _____ .

g) A: Lisa, _____ you play with us after supper?

B: Yes, I _____ . So _____ my sister.

h) A: _____ car salespeople test-drive the cars in the showroom?

B: Yes, they _____ . So _____ prospective buyers.

i) A: _____ company employees park in the front parking lot?

B: Yes, they _____ . So _____ their visitors.

j) A: _____ customers bring pets to that department store?

B: No, they _____ . Neither _____ any of the employees.

k) A: _____ I see you for a moment please?

B: Yes, you _____ . What is it about?

A: The new transaction. I hope we _____ sign the contract today.

l) A: _____ you come to the movies with us tomorrow.

B: I am afraid I _____ . I have no money.

m) A: _____ you change this twenty-dollar bill?

B: Yes, I _____ . Here are four five-dollar bills.

n) A: How do you ask somebody to translate a letter for you?

B: You say: _____ .

A: Is there another way of saying that?

B: Yes, you _____ .

o) A: _____ I go to Flag Place on foot?

B: No, you _____ . It's _____ but you _____ go by bus.

A: Where _____ I catch one?

B: _____ at the corner of Hilltop Street and Eastview Heights Boulevard.

16. Work in pairs. One of you will be the employer and the other will be the applicant for the following positions:

a) a supervisor's job at a department store

b) a teller's position at the Hong Kong Bank of Canada

c) a receptionist's position at Mercedes-Benz of Canada

Remember to make questions with *can*.

UNIT 9 – THE CONTINUOUS TENSES

9.1 SPELLING OF THE PRESENT PARTICIPLE

The **present participle** is the *ing* form of the verb.
a) When a verb ends in a *single e*, drop the *e* and add *ing*.
    close/closing   *move/moving*   *dance/dancing*

b) To an *ee* ending, add *ing*.
    free/freeing   *see/seeing*

c) To a **vowel + single consonant** ending of a **one** syllable verb, double the final consonant and add *ing*.
    knit/knitting   *sit/sitting*   *run/running*

d) To a **vowel + single consonant** ending of a **two or more** syllable verb, double the final consonant and add *ing*, if the stress falls on the last syllable.
    forget/forgetting   *permit/permitting*   *begin/beginning*

But:
    offer/offering   (stress on the first syllable)
    open/opening   (stress on first syllable)
    appear/appearing   (two vowels before final consonant)

When you are not sure of the stress, consult a good dictionary.

9.2 FORMS OF THE PRESENT CONTINUOUS TENSE

AFFIRMATIVE FORM

The affirmative of the present continuous tense is formed with the present tense of auxiliary *be* + the Present Participle form of the verb.
    We **are studying** our grammar lesson.
    I **am drinking** a cup of tea.
    They **are working** on the report.

NEGATIVE FORM

The negative is formed with *not* after the auxiliary verb.

*We **are not doing** anything now.*
*She **is not eating** now.*

INTERROGATIVE FORM

The interrogative is formed by inverting the auxiliary verb and the subject.
*   ***Are** they shopping?*
*   *Why **are** you **leaving**?*

Note: For both the affirmative and negative forms of the present continuous tense, the contractions are the same as those for the present tense of the verb *be*.

*   ***I'm reading** a good story.*
*   ***He's telling** the truth.*
*   ***We're going** to the movies.*
*   *We **aren't working** too hard.*
*   *She **isn't cooking**.*

9.3 SOME USES OF THE PRESENT CONTINUOUS TENSES

a) The present continuous tense is used to express an action happening now, at the moment of speaking.
    *We **are studying** the present continuous tense.*
    *The teacher **is explaining** the lesson to us.*

b) It is used to indicate an action happening at this time, but not at the precise moment of speaking.
    *She **is taking** a sewing course. (these days)*
    *They **are planning** for their wedding. (at the present time)*

c) It is used to express immediate and definite plans.
    ***They're driving** to Montreal tonight.*
    ***She's washing** her hair tonight.*

d) It is used to express a frequently repeated fact or condition that bothers the speaker, or that the speaker admires.
    *He **is always coming in** late to class. (This is annoying me!)*
    *She **is always helping** her little brother with his homework. (I admire this.)*

The meaning of the sentence is made clear by the tone of voice and the context.

*She **is always studying**. (I don't like it!)*

Note: When two verbs in the present continuous tense follow one another, the auxiliary *be* can be omitted with the second verb.

*He's **singing** and **dancing** for the children.*
*The girls are **talking** and **laughing**. They aren't **fighting** or **arguing**.*

9.4 VERBS NOT USED IN THE PRESENT CONTINUOUS TENSE

The following verbs are not normally used in the present continuous tense. Use them, therefore, in the simple present tense instead.

a) Verbs expressing emotion: *care, desire, dislike, forgive, hate, like, love, want, wish*
   *I **hate** pecans.*
   *I **want** another piece of pie.*
   *She doesn't **care** for musicals.*

b) Verbs expressing a point of view: *believe, know, mind, forget, remember, understand, refuse*
   *Do you **know** her?*
   *I don't **believe** she is lying!*

c) Verbs expressing possession: *belong, own, possess, have*
   *He **owns** a piece of land in the mountains.*
   *They **have** two lovely rose bushes.*

d) Verbs expressing a state or condition: *appear, be, seem, look, consist*
   *Did you sleep well last night? You **look** tired.*
   *She **appears** happier today.*
   *The hiring process **consists** of a series of interviews.*

e) Verbs of the senses: *see, hear, smell, taste* and *feel* as a linking verb
   *I **see** a dog in my yard. Whose is it?*
   *The roast beef **smells** really good!*
   *These leather gloves **feel** smooth.*

9.5   SPECIAL MEANINGS OF VERBS IN THE PRESENT CONTINUOUS TENSE

a) A question with **what** and the verb **do** in the present or past continuous means **why**.
What is this hat doing on my desk?
(Why is this hat on my desk?)

What were you doing there in the middle of the night?
(Why were you there in the middle of the night?)

b) Verbs of the senses such as **see**, **hear** and **smell** can be used in the present continuous tense only in the following cases:

- *See* meaning "visit" or "meet by appointment"
I am seeing my grandparents this afternoon.
He is seeing the dentist tomorrow at noon.
- *Hear* meaning "receive news from" or "about"
We are hearing a lot about the elections.
- *Smell* indicating a deliberate action
Why are you smelling the meat? Isn't it fresh?

c) The verbs **be** and **have** are used in the present continuous tense in the following cases:

- When *be* implies that the subject is showing some quality temporarily
The children are being difficult today.
Stop that! You're being silly!
- When *have* does not mean possession or obligation
We are having a good time.
The baby is having a nap.

9.6   FORMS OF THE PAST CONTINUOUS TENSE

AFFIRMATIVE FORM

The affirmative of the **past continuous tense** is formed with the past of the Auxiliary *be* + the Present Participle of the verb.
At this time last year, I was visiting friends in Edmonton.
At nine o'clock last night, I was watching T.V.

NEGATIVE FORM

The negative is formed with *not*.

> He **was not working** when I arrived.
> They **were not having** lunch when she called.

INTERROGATIVE FORM

The interrogative is formed by inverting the auxiliary verb and the subject.

> What **was** she **looking for** when you saw her?
> What **were** you **doing** when I called?

Note: The contractions for the negative form of the past continuous tense are the same as for the past tense of the verb *be*.

> They **weren't** having lunch when she called.
> He **wasn't** working when I arrived.

9.7 USE OF THE PAST CONTINUOUS TENSE

The past continuous tense is never used alone, but always in relation to some other past action, either expressed or understood. It is used to indicate an action that was going on at a specific moment or period of time in the past.

> In 1984, they **were** still **living** in Vancouver.
>
> What **were** you **doing** when the fire alarm went off?
> I **was taking** a bath.
>
> I couldn't talk to him when he called.
> What **were** you **doing**?
> I **was hanging** pictures in my livingroom.

9.8 TIME CLAUSES WITH *WHEN* AND *WHILE*

WHILE

While emphasizes the continuity or duration of an action. It is generally used with a continuous tense to indicate that the action is going on at a certain time.

Carla **is making** the beds **while** her partner **is making** breakfast.
The author **was signing** autographs **while** his friends **were taking** pictures.

While can also be used with a simple tense to show two actions occurring at the same time, and lasting the same length of time.

While Shelisa **makes** breakfast, her husband **sets** the table.
Yesterday, **while** she **ran** to the store, he **made** lunch.

WHEN

When refers to a punctual action or an action of short duration.

When the bell **rang**, the students stopped writing and put their pens down.
When the child **saw** the clown, he began to chuckle.

Note: The simple past tense and the past continuous tense can be used in the same sentence.

The simple past is used for the shorter action of the two, and the past continuous is used to show the continuity of the second action.

The baby **was taking** a nap when the dog **started** to bark.
When I **called** her, she **was getting** dinner ready.
While he **was doing** the dishes, she **put** the children to bed.

9.9   BE GOING TO

FOR FUTURE INTENTION

Be going to in the present continuous + the Infinitive is used to express intention or determination.

Be going to is formed in the same way as the present continuous tense of the verb *go*.

I'm going to travel all over Canada.
My brother **is going to** spend two weeks in Quebec City to learn French.
My parents **aren't going to** travel this summer.
Where **are** you **going to** spend your holidays?

FOR PAST INTENTION

Be going to in the past continuous tense + Infinitive is used to indicate an action that was **planned in the past and did not happen in the past**.

> I **was going to** buy him a present, but I didn't have enough money. I made him a cake instead.

> He **was going to** work on a tobacco farm last summer, but he changed his mind and took a job as a waiter instead.

Was going to is also used to indicate that the action **planned in the past will not happen now or in the future**.

> I **was going to** do some house cleaning now but I'm not feeling well. **I'm going to** lie down for a few minutes.

> They **were going to** join a swimming club this summer, but they decided to rent a cottage instead. They're looking for a cottage on Lake Huron.

9.10 EXERCISES

IMPROVE YOUR SPEAKING AND WRITING

1. Complete the following sentences with the verb provided in the simple present tense or the present continuous tense.

EXAMPLE: Paula **does not have** (not have) a lot of free time. She **is taking** (take) five courses this year and, right now, she **is working** (work) 15 hours a week at a drugstore. She **is** (be) always very busy.

a) Stacey _is_____ (be) in Ramon's Department Store now. She _seems_ (seem) happy and excited. Her youngest daughter _is getting_ (get) married and Stacey _is buying_ (buy) all sorts of things for the engagement party. The store _is offering_ (offer) many good discounts today. The prices ____are____ (be) just terrific! Stacey _is rushing_ (rush) from display to display. She _does not have_ (have) much time. She _is meeting_ (meet) her daughter for lunch in an hour.

b) Why ____is____ (be) the teacher upset at Alphonso? He ____is____ (be) impossible these days! He ____is____ always _talking_ (talk) and ____making____ (make) fun of the other students'

181

mistakes. When he _is not disturbing_ (not disturb) the class, he _is reading_ (read) his comic books. What _is_ (be) his problem? Well, he _has_ (have) many family problems at home. I really _don't know_ (not know) the details. He _doesn't talk_ (talk) much about it. He sure _needs_ (need) help.

c) What _are_ (do) your friends _doing_ these days? Sophia _is driving_ (drive) a cab. Her sister, Julia, _is planning_ (plan) a fund-raising ball for a new retirement home. Arturo _is teaching_ (teach) history at Wilson Secondary School. Paula _is taking_ (take) karate lessons and Julio _is going_ (go) to school. What _is_ (do) their mother _doing_ ? She _is learning_ (learn) English at George Brown College and she _loves_ (love) every minute of it. She has made many friends. They _have_ (have) lunch together, they _go_ (go) to the library, to the movies.... She _is_ just _have_ (have) a ball.

2. **What are these people saying? Follow the example.**

EXAMPLE:

A: What is Laura doing?
B: She is reading a letter.

Laura?
read a letter

a) A: _____ Max and Jack _____ ?
    B: _____

Max and Jack?
watch T.V.

b) A: _____ Tanya _____ ?
    B: _____

Tanya?
play tennis

c) A: _____ you _____ ?

B: _____

d) A: _____ the children _____ ?

B: _____

e) A: _____ Cliff _____ ?

B: _____

f) A: _____ Ann and Juanita _____ ?

B: _____

g) A: _____ your parents _____ ?

B: _____

h) A: _____ your teacher _____ ?

B: _____

i) A: _____ Tony _____ ?

B: _____

j) A: _____ Miranda _____ ?

B: _____

3. Complete the following sentences with the verbs provided in the simple past or the past continuous tense.

EXAMPLE: When the doorbell **rang** (ring), I was **reading** (read) the paper.

a) Elzbietta _____ (lecture) at Waterloo University when she first _____ (meet) her husband.

b) My poor uncle _____ (wash) the kitchen floor when he _____ (slip) and _____ (twist) his ankle.

c) The new housekeeper _____ (scratch) the silver tray while she _____ (clean) it.

d) When you _____ (see) Luciano, _____ he still _____ (wear) his braces?

e) While this poor woman _____ (kill) herself at two jobs, her irresponsible son _____ (waste) her money on extra parts for his motorcycle.

f) Roula _____ (not come) to our party last Saturday. She _____ (work) the night shift and by the time she _____ (finish), it _____ (be) too late.

g) When Sam was a college student, he _____ (support) himself. He _____ (work) and _____ (study) at the same time.

h) My friends _____ (visit) their relatives in Vancouver when their daughter _____ (meet) Rudolfo.

i) I _____ (sand) my old Victorian side table when the leg _____ (come) off.

j) At the airport, they _____ (have) a light snack while they _____ (wait) for their grandmother.

k) While the baby _____ (have) a nap, Rosalia _____ (repair) the broken picture frame.

l) My cousins _____ (save) a lot of money when they _____ (live) with my parents.

m) I _____ still _____ (get) dressed when our first guests _____ (arrive).

4. Combine the following pairs of sentences to create one complex sentence. Use *when* or *while* in the correct position. Make any necessary changes. (See 9.8.)

EXAMPLE: The reporters took notes.

The President was making a speech. (while)

The reporters took notes while the President was making a speech.

a) He discovered a priceless oil painting.

He was cleaning his grandfather's basement. (while)

b) The waiters walked out of the restaurant in protest.

We were still having lunch. (when)

c) Revenue Canada called.

He was picking out furniture for his office. (when)

d) The electricity went off.

The storm began. (when)

e) He accidentally hit and burst a water pipe.

He was digging a big hole for his blue spruce. (when)

f) She fell off the big apple tree.

She was pruning the big apple tree. (while)

g) Wasps stung Peter.

Peter was destroying their nests. (while)

h) Samia shortened her new dress.

She was watching The National on T.V. (while)

i) Stavros was 13 years old.

His family moved to Australia. (when)

j) The shoemaker repaired my sandal.

I waited. (while)

5. Rewrite the following sentences, substituting the past tense form of *going to* for the italicized verbs. (See 9.9.)

EXAMPLE: I *intended* to help her but then I got sick.

I was going to help her but then I got sick.

a) They *intended* to move to a larger apartment but they decided against it.

b) She *wanted* to take up nursing but her final high school marks were too low.

c) We *wanted* to bring our dictionaries to school but then we remembered we couldn't use them during exams.

d) They *planned* to have a very big wedding but now they're putting the money towards a little house.

e) They *intended* to go to the lake for a day of fun in the sun but then it started to rain.

f) The whole family was *ready* to go for a walk in the woods when the grandparents dropped in for a cup of tea.

g) I *planned* to watch *Casablanca* last night but I fell asleep on the couch.

h) We *intended* to paint the garage door this weekend but the weather forecast is for heavy rains.

i) I *wanted* to invite her to a fish barbecue but then I remembered her allergies to fish and seafood.

j) Mr. Cox *planned* to buy a new car but he says now he's going to fix the old one.

6. Complete the following dialogues between Anna and Bea with a verb in the simple present or present continuous tense.

a) A: _____ Cathy _____ (need) tickets for the fashion show?

   B: I _____ (not think) _____ so. She _____ (not like) _____ fashion shows. She _____ (prefer) concerts.

   A: What kind of concerts?

   B: Jazz concerts. As a matter of fact, right now she _____ (attend) a concert by young jazz musicians from New Orleans.

b) A: Did you see Césare last night?

B: No, but I _____ (see) him later on tonight.

A: _____ he _____ (come) to your house?

B: No, we _____ (meet) at the library and from there we _____ (go) to the university auditorium.

A: What _____ (be) on?

B: The third-year political science students _____ (put) on a violin and piano concert.

c) A: How well _____ you _____ (know) the Dulays?

B: Not well. They just contracted us for some remodelling work. Next week, we _____ (paint) the living room and _____ (wallpaper) the bedrooms.

A: They _____ (have) a lovely home, _____ they?

B: Yes, they also _____ (own) a little cottage on Georgian Bay.

d) A: _____ you _____ (apply) for the new position?

B: I _____ (not think) so. I _____ (not have) any experience in that kind of work.

A: Why _____ you _____ (try) anyway?

B: No, Anna. I _____ (not have) the right _____ qualifications either. Besides, I can't have a full-time job. I _____ (go) back to school in September.

EXPRESS YOURSELF

1. Ask a partner the following questions. Your partner will answer with an excuse using *was/were going to* and *but*.

EXAMPLE: Didn't you finish the assignment?

I was going to finish it hours ago but I had too many interruptions.

a) Haven't you make your bed yet?

b) Are you still smoking?

c) Aren't you looking for a job yet?

d) Why don't you buy yourself a good dictionary?

e) Why don't you join a fitness class?

f) Why don't you listen to the doctor and go on a diet?

g) I was waiting for your call yesterday! Why didn't you call?

h) Why did you take my bicycle from the garage without asking me first?

i) I'm mad at you! Why didn't you tell me you stained my coffee table?

j) Why didn't you repair the garage door while it was still daylight?

2. Work with a partner. Your partner will ask you the following questions about what you are doing right now. Give long answers.

a) What are you doing right now?

b) Are you using the blackboard or your exercise book?

c) Where are you sitting?

d) Is anyone else sitting with you in this room?

e) What are you practicing?

f) Are you having trouble with the present continuous tense?

g) Are you having difficulties with this exercise?

h) Is anyone helping you with this exercise?

i) Are you writing down the answers to these questions?

j) Are you using a dictionary?

k) Is the teacher talking to you now?

l) How are you feeling now?

m) Who in particular are you thinking about?

n) Are you drinking a cup of coffee while you're answering these questions?

o) Are you smoking?

p) Are you munching on something?

q) Are you chewing gum?

r) Is any music playing?

s) Is anyone talking?

3. Ask a partner the following questions. Your partner will answer. Then ask three questions of your own, and write them down.

   a) Where are you going after school today?

   b) Where are you having dinner tonight?

   c) What are you having for dinner?

   d) Who are you having dinner with?

   e) When are you going shopping?

   f) How are you spending your evening?

   g) What are you doing this weekend?

   h) Are you seeing someone special?

   i) Are you writing to your family soon?

   j) Are you inviting some people over for dinner? If yes, are you doing the cooking? What are you serving?

   k) When are you writing your final test?

   l) When are you graduating?

   m) Are the students planning a graduation party?

   n) Are you registering for another course?

4. Now your partner will ask you the questions in exercise 3 above. Answer and then write a short paragraph about yourself in the future. Use *be going to* when you can.

5. Work with a partner. Your partner will ask you the following questions about yourself. Give long answers.

   a) Are you enjoying your English course?

   b) Are you reading more English books now than before?

   c) Are you speaking English all the time?

   d) Are you practicing your English?

   e) Is your English improving?

   f) Are you learning many new words?

   g) How are you spending your free time these days?

   h) Are you saving money for a rainy day?

i) Are you enjoying life here?

j) Are you making new friends?

6. Ask your partner the questions in exercise 5 above. Report your partner's answers to the class, then write a short paragraph about what your partner is doing these days.

7. Ask a partner the following questions. Your partner will answer in complete statements.

a) What are you going to do after you finish this course?

b) What are you going to do if you don't pass your English test?

c) What are you going to do next summer?

d) What are you going to do on your next long weekend?

e) Is the teacher going to give you a final test?

f) Are all the students going to pass?

g) Are the teachers going to have a meeting?

h) Is the school going to organize a school dance?

i) Is your best friend going to take a course?

8. Ask a partner the following questions. Your partner will answer in complete statements.

a) What were you doing at this time yesterday?

b) What were you doing at this time last year? Two years ago?

c) Where were you living?

d) Were you studying or working?

e) What were you doing at 5:00 p.m. yesterday?

f) What language were you speaking with your classmate just a few minutes ago?

g) What were you telling him or her?

h) What was the teacher doing when you came into the classroom?

i) What were the students doing?

j) What were the students doing when the latecomers came in?

9. Tell the class and then write down your responses.

    a) Look out the window and describe what people are doing.

    b) Tell the class what the weather is like.

    c) Look around you. What are your classmates doing? What are they wearing?

    d) Name a few of your friends or relatives who are still living in your country. Describe what each one is probably doing.

    e) Tell the class what you're going to do after you finish this course.

    f) Tell the class what you were doing at this time of year in your country.

    g) Tell the class a few things you were going to do yesterday or a few days ago and then decided not to.

10. Did you ever make plans for your future, plans that you couldn't or can't keep? Tell the class. Begin with, "I was going to...".

11. Write a short letter to a friend telling her about your life in your new country.

UNIT 10 – ADVERBS

An adverb is a word that modifies a verb, an adjective, or another adverb.

> *She sings **well**.*
> *Her father owns a **very** big store.*
> *They serve dinner **too** early. I'm never hungry at 6:00 p.m.*

Adverbs are classified according to their function in a sentence.

10.1 ADVERBS OF PLACE

Adverbs of place answer *where* questions about the verb.

Some adverbs of place are *here, there, up, down, upstairs, downstairs* and *downtown*. These adverbs usually follow the verb.

> *These people do not live **here**.*
> *That bus goes **downtown**.*

10.2 ADVERBS OF TIME

Adverbs of time answer *when* questions about the verb.

Adverbs of time, such as *now, then, today, yesterday* and *tomorrow*, usually follow the verb, the direct object or an expression of place. They can also precede the subject and verb, usually for emphasis.

> *He didn't arrive **yesterday**.*
> *We don't need any bread **today**.*
> *We usually go to the computer room but **yesterday** we went to the library.*

10.3 ADVERBS OF DEGREE

Adverbs of degree, such as *very, too, rather, fairly,* and *almost*, usually come before the word they modify.

> *He's **almost** ready.*
> *They came home **rather** late last night.*
> *He's **very** short for his age.*

Note: Hardly is an adverb of degree with a negative meaning of "almost not at all."

*I **hardly** understand my grandfather when he talks to me without his dentures.*
*My aunt can **hardly** see without her glasses.*

Do not confuse *hardly* with *hard*. These two words are not related. The adverb of *hard* is *hard*.

*The residents of the town of Markham fought **hard** against the proposed dump site in their neighbourhood.*

10.4 ADVERBS OF FREQUENCY

Adverbs of frequency, such as *often, never, seldom, always* and *usually*, are placed:
- After the verb *be*
    *They are **never** home on Sunday afternoons.*
- Before other verbs
    *We **usually** go shopping after work on Fridays.*
- Between the auxiliary and the main verb
    *Andrew didn't **always** teach French.*
    *She is **always** enjoying herself.*
    *Did you **often** go to the beach when you lived in Australia?*
    *I can **never** understand him on the phone.*

10.5 ADVERBS OF INTENSITY

Adverbs of intensity, such as *only, just, especially, precisely* and *particularly*, emphasize some particular word or words in a sentence. They precede the word or words they emphasize.

*I came **just** to see you.*
*We should arrive at **exactly** nine o'clock.*
*Naveen found his history class **particularly** boring.*

10.6 ADVERBS OF MANNER

Adverbs of manner usually answer *how* questions about the verb.

*The children behaved **very well** at the wedding.*

FORM

Most adverbs of manner are formed by adding *ly* to the corresponding adjective.

Adjective	Adverb
slow	SLOWLY
quiet	QUIETLY
complete	COMPLETELY

When the adjective ends in *y*, the adverb is formed by changing the *y* to *i* and adding *ly*.

Adjective	Adverb
happy	HAPPILY
lazy	LAZILY
merry	MERRILY

When the adjective ends in *able* or *ible*, the adverb is formed by dropping *e* and adding *y*.

Adjective	Adverb
comfortable	COMFORTABLY
sensible	SENSIBLY
terrible	TERRIBLY

Exceptions:

a)   The adverb corresponding to *good* is *well*.
*He is a **good** singer. He sings **well**.*
Well can also be an adjective when it means "in good health":
*Frank doesn't feel **well** today, he's quite ill.*

b)   *High, low, hard, fast, deep, far, early* and *late* can be used as adjectives or adverbs.
*Fred runs **fast**. He's a **fast** runner.*
*She gets up **early**. She's an **early** riser.*

c)   Adjectives ending in *ly* have no adverb form. A phrase is used instead.
*She is a **friendly** woman. She welcomed us in a **friendly** way.*
*He is a **silly** child. He always acts in a **silly** way.*

d)   Some adverbs have a different meaning from their corresponding adjectives.
*The weather was rather **cold** last week.*
*Why did they act so **coldly**? (in an unfriendly manner)*
*These drapes are definitely too **short**.*
*I expect him **shortly**. (in a little while)*
*The weather was **warm** enough so we went swimming.*
*They always welcome us **warmly**. (in a friendly way)*

POSITION

Adverbs of manner can occur in several positions:
- After the verb, if there is no object in the sentence
*The patient slept **soundly**.*
- Before the verb, if the object of the verb is an infinitive
*I **gradually** learned to speak English.*

The position of some adverbs may affect the meaning of the sentence.
*He **quickly** promised to complete the work. (quickly modifies promised)*
*He **promised** to complete the work quickly. (quickly modifies complete)*

In the first sentence, *quickly* tells how he promised. In the second sentence, *quickly* tells how he will complete the work.

10.7 *HOW* + ADJECTIVE OR ADVERB

How is used with an adjective or an adverb to ask for information.
How old is the baby?
How old is that house?
How well do you speak Cantonese?
My husband drives very slowly. It takes him a long time to get to work.
How slowly does he drive?

10.8 INFORMATION QUESTIONS WITH *HOW*

Information Requested	Response	Example
Manner	Adverb	HOW does he speak? CLEARLY. HOW do they walk? SLOWLY.
State or Condition	Adjective	HOW do you like your coffee? BLACK. HOW do you find Winnipeg? VERY CLEAN.
Means of Transportation	BY + Noun **Exception:** ON FOOT	HOW do you come to school? BY BUS. HOW will she get to Whitehorse? BY PLANE.
Tools or Equipment	WITH + Noun	HOW do you mow the lawn? WITH A LAWNMOWER.
Action: How Something Is Done	BY + ING Form of Verb	HOW did she get the tablecloth so white? BY SOAKING it in water for a few hours.

10.9 EXERCISES

IMPROVE YOUR SPEAKING AND WRITING

1. Write the adverb for each adjective provided. Then complete the sentences with either the adjective or the adverb. (See 10.6.)

EXAMPLE: (noisy) **noisily**

The students held a **noisy** celebration last night. They celebrated their graduation rather **noisily**.

a) (hard)

He was always a _____ worker. He worked very _____ all his life.

b) (exact)

Tell me _____ what you want, then I can quote you the _____ price.

c) (entire)

The politician spoke to the _____ French community. She spoke to them _____ in French.

d) (high)

He has a very _____ position in the firm. His former supervisor _____ recommended him for this job.

e) (good)

Charlie is a _____ pianist! He also plays the banjo very _____ .

f) (prompt)

They expected a very _____ reply to the letter, so I responded _____ by courier.

g) (safe)

It wasn't a very _____ journey, so their parents were ecstatic when they crossed the border _____ .

h) (courageous)

These were very _____ young people. They fought the enemy
and defended their country most _____ .

   i) (elegant)

My aunt is the most _____ woman. No one can dress as
_____ as she.

   j) (considerable)

We put on _____ weight while we were on our holidays. We
went on a diet and now our weight is decreasing _____ .

   k) (poor)

Her parents were very upset at her _____ marks in history. She
always does _____ because she can't memorize dates and
places.

   l) (careful)

Although he usually works _____ , yesterday he wasn't as
_____ and broke two expensive china pots.

   m) (terrible)

My grandfather's food sometimes tastes _____ and I feel
_____ embarrassed when I can't eat it.

   n) (thorough)

The police interviewed the witness _____ . They got a
_____ account of the accident.

   o) (exceptional)

Anna Maria is an _____ talented flutist! She is also an
_____ landscape artist!

2.   What are these people saying? Follow the example.

EXAMPLE:

A: Be careful in your work!

B: Don't worry! I always work carefully.

199

a) A: _____ precise _____
    B: _____

b) A: _____ fast _____
    B: _____

c) A: _____ quiet _____
    B: _____

d) A: _____ creative _____
    B: _____

e) A: _____ diligent _____
    B: _____

f) A: _____ intelligent _____
    B: _____

g) A: _____ industrious _____
    B: _____

h) A: _____ neat _____
    B: _____

i) A: _____ quick _____

   B: _____

j) A: _____ confident _____

   B: _____

k) A: _____ cheerful _____

   B: _____

l) A: _____ honest _____

   B: _____

3. Rewrite the sentences, placing the adverb (or adverbs) provided in the correct position.

EXAMPLE: Barbers and hairdressers are open on Saturdays. (generally)

   Barbers and hairdressers are generally open on Saturdays.

   a) They open on Sundays. (never)

   b) They close on Mondays and Wednesdays. (usually)

   c) They are open six days a week. (sometimes)

   d) Students go to the cafeteria at lunchtime. (always)

   e) They spend their coffee breaks in the library. (sometimes)

   f) They can eat or drink in the library. (never)

   g) Some students come to school early. (often)

   h) My students come late. (seldom)

   i) I go to the library after class. (sometimes)

j) I borrow books. (often)

k) I return them before the due date. (always)

l) I handle my library books. (carefully)

m) I can finish a book in a few days. (never)

n) I read my book so that I can understand it. (slowly) (well)

o) I prepare my work and check my spelling. (thoroughly) (always)

p) I use the dictionary and ask the teacher. (regularly) (occasionally)

4. Rewrite the sentences, placing the adverb (or adverbs) provided in the correct position.

EXAMPLE: The children are in the park. (still)

The children are still in the park.

a) My English is poor. (rather)

b) I am studying English, no other subject. (just)

c) I started school (just) so I don't speak English. (fluently, yet)

d) My English classes begin at nine o'clock. (exactly)

e) This course is difficult (somewhat), but I am working (hard) and learning. (fast)

f) My teacher is experienced (very). She can answer any grammar question (almost, well) and without hesitation.

g) My teacher is strict and punctual. (particularly)

h) She doesn't like noisy students or lazy ones. (particularly)

i) She tolerates absenteeism. (hardly)

j) She starts her class at nine o'clock (precisely) and we work without a pause (almost) until coffee break.

k) She is as fussy about spelling. (nearly)

l) Last month, she failed my friend George (almost) for his spelling mistakes.

m) George was in tears (nearly). He dropped out of the course. (almost)

n) George lost marks for spelling errors. (only)

o) Everybody else did well. His was the low mark. (only) He doesn't apply

himself! (just) He has no interest in grammar or spelling. (almost)
Tennis is his interest. (only)

p) Yolanda is sitting in the back of the class. She says she can hear the
teacher. (hardly)

5. Create a question with *How* or *How* + an Adjective for each of
the statements below. (See 10.7 and 10.8.)

EXAMPLE: She works quietly.

How does she work?

He drives 60 km per hour.

How fast does he drive?

a) He looks younger in short hair.

b) You can make a salad dressing by mixing oil, vinegar and some spices.

c) We enjoyed our trip very much.

d) This chocolate cake tastes delicious!

e) I like my English course very much.

f) The offer sounded rather dishonest.

g) He cut his costs by doing the work himself.

h) The cargo train runs just once a day.

i) Our City Hall is just 10 years old.

j) The movie was only 75 minutes long.

k) They improved the ventilation by installing larger fans.

l) The new soprano's performance was wonderful.

m) The plumber will come as soon as possible.

n) The rope is 2 cm thick.

o) The silk fabric is only 125 cm wide.

p) The main shopping district is 20 minutes from here.

q) You can remove this nail with pliers.

r) Wieslek can run 90 m in 14 seconds.

s) I need two cups of milk for the rice pudding.

t) I also need three eggs.

u)   My apartment building is four floors high.

v)   The air conditioner is working efficiently now.

w)   He got a speeding ticket this morning.

x)   I worked an average of 50 hours a week.

6.   Rewrite the following sentences, placing the words and phrases provided in their correct positions.

EXAMPLE: She arranged the flowers.

(always, attractively, in the shop window)

She always arranged the flowers attractively in the shop window.

a)   They sit.

(after dinner, outside, often, when the weather is mild)

b)   They found a job.

(in Scarborough, finally, good)

c)   She is staying.

(today, to finish her assignment, home)

d)   The whole family came.

(two years ago, here, exactly)

e)   She went.

(after lunch, to water her plants, outside)

f)   She left her glasses.

(almost, today, at work)

g)   Take the empty cups.

(right, now, to the kitchen)

h)   Could you please read the instructions?

(once, at least, carefully)

i)   Our guests arrived.

(at the restaurant, yesterday, early)

j)   They went.

(for a swim, always, to the lake)

k)   Peter waited.

(at the door, patiently, for several minutes)

l)   Luba left.

(after dinner, immediately, while it was still light)

EXPRESS YOURSELF

1.   Ask a partner the following questions. Your partner will answer with short responses beginning with *by* + the *ing* form of the verb.

EXAMPLE: How can people become instant millionaires?

By winning at the lottery.

a)   How can people reduce the quantity of their garbage?

b)   How can manufacturing companies help the environment?

c)   How can people have very white teeth?

d)   How can people keep in shape?

e)   How can we protect ourselves from the sun's rays?

f)   How can we keep well-informed?

g)   How can runners become very fast?

h)   How can people travel cheaply?

i)   How can you save on clothes?

j)   How can one save on maintenance bills?

k)   How can stores attract new customers?

l)   How can drivers avoid trouble on the road?

m)   How do car manufacturers test cars?

n)   How do cooks test new recipes?

2.   Ask a partner the following questions. Your partner will answer in complete statements that include an adverb.

EXAMPLE: How do you file your recipes?

I file them alphabetically.

a)   How do most drivers drive on the highway?

b)   How do advertisements usually describe an item?

c)   How do people usually act in a temple, mosque or church?

d) How do sports fans act at games, especially when the team is winning?

e) How often do people get paid?

f) How often do people receive their newspaper?

g) How do parents hold their baby?

h) How does your teacher speak?

i) How do you usually do on your tests or exams?

j) How do you handle delicate crystal?

3. Ask a partner the following questions. Your partner will answer in complete statements that include an adjective.

a) How do North Americans drink their milk?

b) How do Latin Americans like their seafood?

c) How do some teenagers wear their hair?

d) How do you like your coffee?

e) How do you make your coffee or tea? Strong or weak?

f) How do you eat your meat? Rare, medium or well done?

g) Do you eat potatoes? How do you prefer them?

h) Do you like eggs? How do you like them?

i) How do you keep your bedroom?

j) When you left home this morning, how did you leave your kitchen?

k) How do you find English?

l) How do you find your E.S.L. course?

m) How do you find life in this place?

4. Ask a partner the following questions. Your partner will answer with short responses beginning with *by* or *with* + a Noun. Then ask a few questions of your own, and write them down.

a) How do you come to school?

b) How do you keep in touch with your family?

c) How do you pay your bills?

d) How can you find your way around a new city?

e) How can you travel from one country to another?

f) How do you wash your kitchen floor?

g) How do you draw a straight line?

h) How do you make a perfect circle?

i) How do you remove food stains from clothes?

j) How do you clean glass windows?

k) How do you remove oil paint from the floor?

l) How do we keep our homes warm in winter?

m) How do we keep our homes cool in summer?

n) How can I thin paint?

o) How can I thicken gravy?

p) How can I tell a genuine precious stone from a synthetic one?

q) How do we begin a letter in English?

r) How do you begin a letter in your language?

s) How can I make a simple salad dressing?

t) How do welders weld two pieces of metal?

5. Make statements about yourself using the verb/adverb combinations as suggested below. Make your sentences more informative by adding words or phrases of time or place when possible.

EXAMPLE: spend/usually

I usually spend my weekends at the provincial park when the weather is nice.

a) buy/just

b) eat/never

c) do/carefully

d) spend/only

e) understand/well

f) write/regularly

g) work/always

h) learn/still

      i)   be/often

      j)   study/hard

      k)   leave/fast

      l)   miss/almost

First work with a partner. Then write out all your sentences.

6.   Class Activity: Each student will pick a place of interest in the city or country, and ask a partner a question with *how* + an Adjective (*how far, how long, how wide*, and so on). If the partner doesn't know the answer, she or he should reply, "I'm sorry, I don't know" or "I have no idea." After that, another student will ask a partner a question and so on, until the whole class has had a turn.

EXAMPLE: How far is City Hall from your house?

It is about 10 km from my house.

OR

I'm sorry, I don't know.

UNIT 11 – DIRECT AND INDIRECT OBJECT PATTERNS

11.1 TO AND FOR BEFORE INDIRECT OBJECTS

STRUCTURE 1

Subject	+	Verb	+	Direct Object	+	To	+	Indirect Object
They		gave		a bonus		to		the workers.
He		offered		a red rose		to		each participant.

The verbs used in this structure include *promise, take, bring, give, send, lend, pay, offer, tell, show, hand, sell, grant* and *loan.*

STRUCTURE 2

Subject	+	Verb	+	Direct Object	+	For	+	Indirect Object
They		bought		some gifts		for		the children.
They		built		a house		for		their new puppy.

The verbs used in this structure include *buy, get, order, make, build, do, cook* and *save.*

Note: Both Structure 1 and Structure 2 have an alternative form. **The indirect object is placed before the direct object** and the preposition *to* or *for* is omitted.

> *They gave a bonus* **to the workers.**
> *They gave* **the workers** *a bonus.*
>
> *He offered a red rose* **to each participant.**
> *He offered* **each participant** *a red rose.*
>
> *They bought some gifts* **for the children.**
> *They bought* **the children** *some gifts.*
>
> *They built a house* **for their new puppy.**
> *They built* **their new puppy** *a house.*

This construction is more common, but it is not used when:
• The direct object is a pronoun

210

*He paid **the rent to the landlord.***
*He paid **the landlord the rent.***
***But**: He paid **it** to the landlord. (no alternative possible)*

- When both the direct and indirect objects are pronouns

*He paid **it** to **him**. (no alternative possible)*

STRUCTURE 3

Subject	+ Verb	+ Direct Object	+ To	+ Indirect Object
Georges	spoke	English	to	Marie.
We	said	good morning	to	the teacher.
The waiter	suggested	fish	to	the customer.

This structure has no alternative form. The preposition *to* is always used before the indirect object with the following verbs: *explain, describe, introduce, speak, say, mention, complain, report, announce, suggest* and *donate*.

STRUCTURE 4

Subject	+ Verb	+ Indirect Object	+ Direct Object
They	wished	us	good luck.
We	asked	the witness	many questions.
She	paid	the real estate broker	two thousand dollars.

A preposition is never used before the indirect object with the following verbs: *ask, cost, charge, pay, save* and *wish*. With these verbs, the indirect object comes before the direct object.

11.2 VERBS FOLLOWED BY *TO* INFINITIVE

Subject	+ Verb	+ *To* Infinitive
Rona	hopes	TO SPEAK English fluently soon.
They	decided	TO SELL the farm.
Gus	wants	TO APPLY for the position.

The verbs used in this structure are *hope, promise, refuse, decide, want, need, agree, try, learn* and *seem*.

11.3 VERBS FOLLOWED BY GERUND

The **gerund** has exactly the same form as the present participle. We form it by adding *ing* to the infinitive. (See section 9.1 for spelling rules.)

The gerund and the present participle have different functions. Whereas the present participle functions as a verb form, the gerund functions as a noun.

Subject	+ Verb	+ Gerund
I	avoid	DRIVING during rush hour.
Do you	enjoy	WINDOW SHOPPING.
I	don't mind	CHANGING seats with you.
She	is considering	QUITTING her job

The verbs in this structure are *finish, avoid, risk, admit, deny, enjoy, keep* (continue), *mind* (object), *miss, consider, stop* (cease), *practice, imagine* and *dread*.

Note: Mind is mainly used in the negative and interrogative.

*Do you **mind waiting** outside?*

*I don't **mind writing** the report by hand.*

Would you mind and *do you mind* are also ways of making a request.

> **Would you mind opening** the door? (Please open the door.)
> **Would you mind moving** a little to the left? I can't see the blackboard.
> **Do you mind repeating** the instructions? I didn't get them.

11.4 SPECIAL EXPRESSIONS FOLLOWED BY GERUND

The gerund is used after the following verbal expressions:

a) *Can't stand* (tolerate), *can't help* (prevent, avoid), *put off*, *it's no use* and after the adjective *worth*
   *Sally **can't stand driving** in winter.*
   *She **can't help feeling** homesick.*
   *It's **no use talking** to her about winter sports! She's not interested.*
   *This movies is not **worth watching**.*

b) *Have trouble, have difficulty, have a hard time, have a difficult time, have fun*
   *Sa Tran **has trouble pronouncing** the r sound.*
   *She **has difficulty reading** long sentences.*
   *She **has a hard time understanding** spoken English.*
   *But she **has fun meeting** new friends.*

c) *Spend* + Time Expression
   *Kerina **spends** an hour a day **practicing** new words.*
   *She **spends** a great deal of her free time **reading** English books.*

d) *Be used to* (be accustomed to), *get used to* (become accustomed to)
   *She's **used to wearing** high heels.*
   *Did they **get used to living** in the Yukon?*

11.5 GERUNDS AS OBJECTS OF A PREPOSITION

A gerund is used if it follows **immediately after** a preposition.

*He's very good **at telling** jokes.*
*She's fond **of swimming**.*
*They're used **to working** hard.*
*He is responsible **for supervising** the office.*
*How **about going** for a walk?*
*She insisted **on wearing** a hat.*
*They thought **of moving** to the city.*
*We didn't look forward **to writing** the math exam.*
***After robbing** the bank, the thief left the country.*
*They help charities **by selling** baked goods.*
*He was accused **of impersonating** a police officer.*

Note: a)   *To* can be either a preposition or part of an infinitive. It is a preposition when it is followed by a noun, a pronoun or a gerund.

*I am looking forward **to** next Christmas/it/visiting Quebec.*
*I am used **to** the heat/it/getting up early.*

Otherwise, *to* is part of the infinitive of the verb.

I love apples.
*I love **to eat** apples.*

I tried on the coat.
*I tried **to mend** the coat.*

      b)   Some verbs can be used in both a *to* + object and a *for* + object structure, with different meanings. *To* implies "directed to/towards." *For* implies "instead of." Compare the following pairs of sentences.

*I paid the bill **to this waiter**. (This waiter got the money.)*
*I paid his bill **for him**. (He didn't have money so I paid his bill.)*

*My mother wanted to know what was in my letter so I read it **to her**.*
*She didn't have her glasses with her so I read the poem **for her**.*

11.6 VERBS + *TO* INFINITIVE OR GERUND — NO CHANGE IN MEANING

Some verbs can be used with either a *to* infinitive or a gerund, with no change in meaning. These verbs are *begin, start, continue, can't bear, love, like, hate, intend,* and *prefer.*

> He began **digging/to dig** a hole.
> They hate **working/to work** on Sundays.
> They started **climbing/to climb** the tree.
> Squirrels love **eating/to eat** peanuts.

Note:

a)   After *intend, can't bear* and *continue*, infinitives are more common.

> We **intend to travel** by plane.
> They **can't bear to travel** by ship.
> He **continued to listen** to the radio.

b)   When *like* means "think right" or "think it a good idea," it is always followed by an infinitive. When it means "enjoy," it is followed by a gerund.

> She **likes to give** to charity. (She thinks it is right to do it.)
> She **likes giving** to charity. (She enjoys giving to charity.)

> I **don't like to tell** lies. (I don't think it is right to do it.)
> I **don't like telling** lies. (I don't enjoy telling lies.)

c)   *Would like* and *would love* have the same meaning as *want*, and are followed only by the infinitive. After a pronoun, *would like* is contracted to *'d like*.

> I'**d like** a cup of coffee. (I want a cup of coffee.)
> They **would like to see** the movie. (They want to see the movie.)
> Martine **would love to see** Rome. (Martine wants to see Rome.)
> **Would** you **like to join** us for coffee? (Do you want to join us for coffee?)

Sometimes, we use **would like** to make a request more polite. *I'd like to speak to George* is more polite than *I want to speak to George*. The interrogative form is *Would you like...?*

> **Would you like to go** to the Art Gallery?
> I'**d love to.**

11.7 VERBS + *TO* INFINITIVE OR GERUND — CHANGE IN MEANING

Some verbs can be used with either a *to* infinitive or a gerund, but the meaning changes.

REGRET/REMEMBER

In ***regret/remember* + gerund**, the action of the verb expressed by the gerund **precedes** *regret* or *remember*.

*I **remembered meeting** her at the party. (I met her at the party and now I remember).*
*I **regretted going** to the party. (I went to the party and then I was sorry.)*

Note: The use of *regret* in this structure is not common. Instead, one would say, *I'm sorry I went to the party.*

In ***regret/remember* + to infinitive**, the action of the verb expressed by the infinitive **follows** *regret* or *remember*.

*He **regretted to tell** you the news. (He regretted before he told it.)*
*He **remembered to buy** the paper. (He remembered, then he bought it.)*

STOP

***Stop* + Gerund** means "cease."
*He **stopped calling** her. (He doesn't call her anymore.)*

Stop can also be followed by a ***to* infinitive of purpose**.
*He **stopped to answer** the door. (Why did he stop? To answer the door.)*

FORGET

***Forget* + *to* Infinitive** means to "not remember" to do something.
*We **forgot to pay** him back for the pictures. (We didn't pay him back because we forgot).*

***Forget* + Gerund** means to "not remember" that one has done something.

We **forgot owing** him money for the pictures. (*We forgot that we owed him money.*

Note: Although a gerund structure with *forget* is correct, it is not commonly used. A *that* clause is used instead.

*I **forgot that** I owed him money for the pictures.*

TRY

Try + *to* Infinitive means "attempt, make the effort."
*The teacher gave us the passage and asked us **to try to understand** it without the dictionary.*

Try + Gerund means "experiment."
The stain wouldn't come out with soap, so he tried scrubbing it with a cleansing powder.

PROPOSE

Propose + *to* Infinitive means "intend."
*I **propose to** end this discussion. (I intend to end it.)*

Propose + Gerund means "suggest."
*I **propose ending** this discussion. (I suggest we end it.)*

MEAN

Mean + *to* Infinitive means "intend."
*He **meant to tell** you what he wanted. (He intended to tell you.)*

Mean + Gerund (with an impersonal subject only) means "involve."
*She is determined to pass the exam even if **it means studying** all night. (...even if it involves studying all night.)*

BE AFRAID

Be afraid + *to* Infinitive means the subject is too afraid to perform the action of the infinitive.
*I **was afraid to show** my ignorance, so I didn't say anything.*

Be afraid of **+ Gerund** expresses plain fear.
> *She is afraid of driving alone at night.*

Used to **+ infinitive** indicates a habitual past action. (See Unit 7.)
To be used to **+ Gerund** means to be accustomed to."
> *He **used to be** fat, but now he's slim.*
> *Are they **used to living** in a tropical climate? (Did they get accustomed to the tropical climate?)*

11.8 GERUNDS WITH POSSESSIVE ADJECTIVES

Since gerunds are used as nouns, they can be modified by possessive adjectives in the same way that nouns are.

Note the difference in meaning in the following pairs of sentences.
> *Do you mind opening the window? (Please open the window.)*
> *Do you mind **my** opening the window? (Do you mind if I open the window?)*

> *I do not recall mentioning this fact. (I do not recall if I mentioned this fact.)*
> *I do not recall **her** mentioning this fact. (I do not recall if she mentioned this fact.)*

> *I enjoy singing in the morning. (I sing in the morning and I enjoy that.)*
> *I enjoy **his** singing in the morning. (He sings in the morning and I enjoy that.)*

11.9 REFLEXIVE PRONOUNS

Reflexive pronouns are object pronouns that refer back to the subject of the verb. In other words, the subject and the reflexive pronoun are the same. They end in **-self** if the subject is singular, and **-selves** if the subject is plural.

I	know	MYSELF.	We	know	OURSELVES.
You	know	YOURSELF.	You	know	YOURSELVES.
He	knows	HIMSELF.			
She	knows	HERSELF.	They	know	THEMSELVES.

*I look at **myself** in the mirror.*
*They can easily hurt **themselves** in that game.*
*She enjoyed **herself** at the party.*

Reflexive pronouns are also used for emphasis, and in this case, they are generally placed after the verb, the direct object, or at the end of the sentence.

Who did the marketing manager send to the convention?
*No one. He went **himself**.*

Who made Mary's dress?
*No one. She made it **herself**.*

These two students are very talented.
*They built the model plane **themselves**.*

Did Ramzi really understand the instructions?
*Yes! I explained them to him **myself**.*

11.10 EXERCISES

IMPROVE YOUR SPEAKING AND WRITING

1. Rewrite the following sentences, changing the italicized word into a pronoun and placing it in the correct position.

EXAMPLE: George lends his truck *to his neighbours*.

George lends them his truck.

a) Saritsa made a summer dress for *Mrs. Robinson*.

b) The shoe exporter mailed *the order* to the customer.

c) Did the secretary report *the accident* to *the manager*?

d) Can the receptionist cash this cheque for *the guests*?

e) They sent *the paints* directly to the warehouse.

f) The Yongs bought toys for *all their grandchildren*.

g) The doctor explained *the case* to *the nurses*.

h) Anna always buys flowers for *her favourite Aunt Louisa*.

i) This company makes *uniforms* for the prisoners.

j) For Mother's Day, the children in my sister's class are making their mothers *paper flowers*.

k) The cook is making *a strawberry cake* for our visitors.

l) Renaldo is going to show his neighbours *his wedding pictures*.

m) My friends are going to write a long letter *to their old friends in Portugal*.

n) I'm sending my mother *some lilies* at Easter.

o) Last night, I read our *parents' letter* to *my sister* over the phone.

p) This teacher often tells *her students* a couple of jokes at the end of the day.

q) I finally agreed to lend my brother *my computer*.

r) At home, Anatoly and Svetlana speak Ukrainian *to their children*.

2. What are these people saying? Follow the example.

EXAMPLE:

A: Are you calling John?

B: No, I'm not calling him. I am calling Carmen.

a) A: _____ phone Peter?

B: _____

b) A: _____ look for Susan?

B: _____

c) A: _____ take Sam and Paul to the park?

    B: _____

d) A: _____ listen to Mozart?

    B: _____

e) A: _____ watch *The Journal*?

    B: _____

f) A: _____ wash your sweaters?

    B: _____

g) A: _____ scold Robbie?

    B: _____

h) A: _____ help your neighbour?

    B: _____

i) A: _____ write to Pam?

    B: _____

j) A: _____ coach the soccer players?

    B: _____

3. Create questions that ask for the italicized information.

EXAMPLE: The volunteer workers made souvenirs for *the guests*.

Who did the volunteer workers make the souvenirs for?

a) They gave *all their employees* some extra time off.

b) She decided to borrow money from *her uncle*.

c) The students in my previous class came from *Bulgaria*.

d) We paid the bills to *the contractor*.

e) She made *us* a turkey dinner.

f) He delivered the flyers to *all his neighbours*.

g) We are buying an extra ticket for *our cousin*.

h) She read me her letter from *her boyfriend*.

i) I decided to report the incident to *the police*.

j) The history teacher is going to show *the students* a documentary on World War II.

k) They are saving money for *their children's education*.

l) I'm sending *my sister* in Australia an art book.

m) She's making *little Carolina* a red winter coat with a matching hat.

4. Complete the following sentences with the correct tense or form of the verbs provided. (See 11.2 and 11.3.)

EXAMPLE: It was just beginning **to rain** (rain) when we **got** (got) into town.

a) The sewing machine is too noisy! I think it needs _____ (oil).

b) I just can't stand _____ (work) in a room without windows.

c) Do you mind _____ (take) off your hat?

d) The delivery truck started _____ (give) them problems so they decided _____ (trade) it in for a newer model.

e) I'm sorry I wasn't paying attention. Would you mind _____ (repeat) the question?

f) "When everybody stops _____ (talk), I will start _____ (teach)," the teacher said angrily.

g) My son spends all his money _____ (treat) his friends to ice cream, so I naturally refused _____ (increase) his weekly allowance.

h) The manager of the corner milk store doesn't keep the store very clean, so we _____ (stop/shop) there.

i) Tom and Esmeralda find the cost of living too high in the city so they are considering _____ (move) to the country.

j) Oswaldo! It's no use _____ (come) to school if you don't have any interest in _____ (improve) your English.

k) Did your South African friends get used to _____ (live) in the Northwest Territories?

l) Do you mind my _____ (call) you back at 10:00 p.m.? I need _____ (speak) to Rosa urgently.

m) Selim doesn't have any experience in _____ (raise) chinchillas, but he decided _____ (start, breed) them anyway.

n) Leon apologized to us for _____ (ask) us personal questions. He didn't mean _____ (look into) our affairs. He was just interested in _____ (help) us.

o) Lucy avoids _____ (park) her car in the underground garage when she gets home late. She prefers _____ (park) on the street.

p) We finished _____ (paint) the bedrooms, but we need _____ (wallpaper) the living room now.

q) Did you forget _____ (mail) the cheque? The contractor just called!
I certainly did not. I remember distinctly _____ (register) it and _____ (mail) it at the post office.

r) Can you please remind your father _____ (send) us his article on red-masked parrots?

s) I am going to invite Stasi _____ (speak) at our next annual meeting.

t) I advised him _____ (start) _____ (save) money and stop _____ (count) on his father _____ (lend) him the necessary funds.

u) We can't help _____ (wonder) about Hiroko's new boss. He never stops _____ (talk) to any of his employees.

5. Complete the following sentences with reflexive pronouns. (See 11.9.)

EXAMPLE: He enjoyed **himself** a lot on the trip.

a) Paul is teaching _____ Russian.

b) Did you enjoy _____ at the picnic?

c) Yesterday, I cut _____ while slicing some green peppers.

d) Don't blame _____ for that misunderstanding! It wasn't your fault.

e) Aunt Yvonne is 87 years old. She can't take care of _____ anymore.

f) Paula burnt _____ when she was taking the potatoes out of the oven.

g) It was cold, so we dried _____ quickly after our swim!

h) I am making _____ a new dress for my cousin's party.

i) How are you preparing _____ for tomorrow's interview?

j) They looked at _____ in the hall mirror before going in the living room.

k) It's unfortunate, but Nora can only think of _____ .

l) You should put _____ in my shoes and try to understand me.

m) I had locked _____ out of the house so I called a locksmith.

6. Complete the following sentences with appropriate reflexive pronouns.

EXAMPLE: Who baked your birthday cake for you?

Nobody, I baked it **myself**.

a) Who is going to clean your windows?

Nobody, we are going to clean them _____ .

b) Are they having a painter paint their house?

No, they aren't. They are painting it _____ .

c) Does she need a carpenter to repair the closet door?

No, she doesn't. She is going to repair it _____ .

d) Who gave you this ceramic flower pot?

Nobody, I bought it _____ .

e) Do you want me to carry that bag for you?

No, thank you. I can carry it _____ .

f) Can you tell the children to play quietly?

Why don't you tell them _____ .

g) Who did Lucy go to the movies with?

Nobody. She went by _____ .

h) Did an interior decorator decorate your living room?

No, I decorated it _____ .

i) Aren't you hungry?

Yes, I am. I am going to help _____ now.

j) Who planned their trip?

Nobody. They planned it _____ .

k) Did you knit this sweater for Mara?

No, she knitted it _____ .

l) Who repaired the wooden deck for Nino?

Nobody. He repaired it _____ .

m) Who showed Laura how to do it?

Nobody. She figured it out _____ .

n) Did Persa type this letter for you?

No, I typed it _____ .

o) Who shovelled the snow on the driveway?

Nobody. I shovelled it _____ .

7. The following are short dialogues between Xenia and Roula. Fill in the missing information using the suggested words.

EXAMPLE: Xenia: My future mother-in-law wanted to see my house.

Roula: So what did you do?

Xenia: (show) **I showed it to her.**

a) X: She needed a dictionary but she didn't have one.

R: So what did you do?

X: (lend)

b) X: I called my family in Turkey this morning.

R: Why?

X: (tell/news about...)

c) X: The dressmaker shortened my red dress and took out the collar.

R: How much did she charge you?

X: (charge $50)

d) X: She wanted a bicycle very badly.

R: Did she get one?

X: (Yes, Uncle Richard/buy)

e) X: I needed an English/Polish dictionary.

R: So what did you do?

X: (borrow/Bozena)

f) X: I decided to paint the kitchen myself.

R: Why?

X: (save)

g) X: The children in my class loved the song.

R: So what did you do?

X: (teach)

h) X: Rena has a beautiful collection of rare orchids.

R: Did you really like them?

X: Yes, as a matter of fact, I (ask, sell me...)

i) X: You look worried! What's wrong?

R: I forgot (lock...)

j) X: It was my sister's birthday!

R: What (buy)?

X: I (just send...)

k) X: Would you like to go to the movies?

R: Not really. I hate (be indoors when...)

X: What about...?

l) X: Any plans for the future?

R: As a matter of fact, I (consider...)

X: What a coincidence! I (think of...)

m) X: What are you doing this weekend?

R: (just want)

X: Would you like...?

8. Complete the following sentences with a direct and an indirect object. Use the prepositions *to* or *for* when necessary.

EXAMPLE: Fazia usually gives **me good advice**.

a) Pierre built _____

b) They decided to stay home and make _____

c) Last Sunday, mother cooked _____

d) Their boss never gave _____

e) At the end of the course, teachers usually give _____

f) This weekend, Branco is going to buy _____

g) At the reception, the Master of Ceremony introduced

_____

h) Because he was on a reducing diet, she didn't offer _____

i) On the whole, the trip cost _____

j) If you're short of money, I can lend _____

k) For all his plumbing work, we paid _____

l) There was an error on our Visa statement so we reported

_____

m) One of the bank's functions is to loan _____

n) Banks also invest _____

o) By making her own clothes, Pina can save _____

p) Please don't mention _____

q) He didn't understand the instructions so I explained _____

r) At his farewell party, all his colleagues wished _____

s) At bedtime, some parents read _____

t) This farmer has four horses and she feeds _____

u) Last Christmas, I sent _____

v) This afternoon, the history instructor is showing _____

9. Work with a partner. Ask your partner the following questions. Your partner will answer using a reflexive pronoun and the suggested words. Add your own words when necessary.

EXAMPLE: What do you do when you're hungry? (make a sandwich)

I make myself a sandwich.

a) What can you do if you feel like having some spicy food? (cook some chicken curry)

b) What can I do if I don't have time to cook? (order a pizza or some Chinese food)

c) What's Nazim doing these days? (build a desk)

d) What did Carla do on her summer holidays? (teach bicycle repair)

e) Why did your boss give up driving to work? (save money on repairs and parking)

f) What did Malia use her yearly bonus for? (buy a new T.V. stand)

g) What is Mrs. Liang teaching the diabetic patients? (give an injection)

EXPRESS YOURSELF

1. Ask your partner the following questions. Your partner will answer with long answers, using a direct and an indirect object.

EXAMPLE: Who did you explain the situation to?

I explained the situation to my first cousin Lena.

a) How often do you write to your family?

b) Do you ever send your family photographs or parcels?

c) Are they sending you a parcel soon?

d) What questions do they ask you in their letters?

e) What do they wish you in their letters?

f) Before an exam, what do your friends wish you?

g) When you registered for this course, what did the interviewer ask you?

h) Did you pay the school any registration fees?

i) Did the school charge you any tuition fees?

j) Does the school charge you a fee for supplies or materials?

k) Is this course costing you any money?

l) Who do you pay your rent to and when?

m) If you have problems with the plumbing or lights, who do you complain to?

n) Are you buying yourself something soon?

o) Did you offer a friend something lately?

p) Did you make something for a friend lately?

q) Do you ever offer your seat on the bus to somebody?

2. Ask a partner the following questions. Your partner will answer in complete statements.

a) Did you every try to learn another language besides English?

b) Do you practice speaking English outside the classroom?

c) Do you need to work while you're taking this course?

d) What do you hope to do in the future?

e) What do you want to achieve in your life?

f) What are you looking forward to?

g) Are you used to living here yet?

h) What do you enjoy doing in your spare time?

i) When your friends need you, do you mind giving up your free time to help them?

j) What are the English letters that you have trouble pronouncing?

k) Do you have difficulty understanding native speakers of English?

l) How many hours a day do you spend studying English? Watching T.V.?

m) What do you hope to achieve by the end of this course?

3. Complete the following sentences about yourself using a gerund, a *to* infinitive or a Noun + Infinitive structure. Make the sentence more informative by adding adverbs and words or phrases of time and place.

EXAMPLE: In winter, I like **to spend my weekends skiing in Horseshoe Valley**.

a) In winter, I like...

b) In summer, I enjoy...

c) On weekends, I prefer...

d) I don't particularly enjoy...

e) After I finish this course, I intend...

f) This afternoon, I'd like...

g) My father taught...

h) The teacher always asks...

i) When I am at school, I try not...

j) In general, I can't stand...

k) When I was a child, I used...

l) Every day, I practice...

m) I always avoid...

n) I often put off...

o) I have trouble...

p) Sometimes, I have difficulty...

q) Yesterday, I spent some time...

r) I am not very good at...

s) Now I don't feel like...

t) Sometimes, I regret...

4.   Tell a partner about the things:
     a)   you are afraid of
     b)   you are terrified of
     c)   you worry about
     d)   you never worry about

Remember to use a gerund after the preposition. After working with your partner, write a paragraph about your feelings.

5.   Which is the most important holiday in your country?
     a)   Tell the class what it is about or what is being celebrated.

     b)   Tell the class how people celebrate this holiday. Explain what people do for one another in celebration. Use verbs such as *mail, send, give, make, prepare, cook* and *donate*.

EXAMPLE: During Ramadan, it is customary to donate money or food to the poor.

UNIT 12 – THE COMPARATIVE AND SUPERLATIVE FORMS

12.1 THE COMPARATIVE FORM OF ADJECTIVES

The **comparative form** is used to compare two elements in size, shape, age, weight, quantity or quality.

*The oak tree on my street is **taller than** the pine tree on First Avenue.*

*An armchair is **more comfortable than** a wooden chair.*

Note: *Than* is part of the comparative form and can be omitted if it is understood.

How did the sweater fit?
*It was too small. I need a **larger** one.*

SHORT ADJECTIVES OF ONE SYLLABLE

If the adjective ends in *e*, add *r*.
*large, **larger***
*wide, **wider***
*late, **later***
*nice, **nicer***
*This belt is too narrow. I need a **wider** one.*
*My kitchen is **larger** than yours.*

If the adjective ends in a single consonant, double the consonant and add *er*.
*big, **bigger***
*hot, **hotter***
*fat, **fatter***
*Yesterday was **hotter** than today.*
*Your house is **bigger** than my brother's.*

If the adjective does not end in *e*, add *er*.
*not young, **younger***
*poor, **poorer***
*small, **smaller***
*rich, **richer***
Are you driving to Chicago?
*No, I'm taking the train. It is **faster**.*

*My bedroom is **smaller than** my den.*

ADJECTIVES ENDING IN Y

If the adjective is one or two syllables and ends in *y*, change *y* to *ier*.

sunny, **sunnier**
happy, **happier**
pretty, **prettier**
busy, **busier**
dry, **drier**
The stores are usually **busier** at Christmas **than** at any other time.
Clarissa just moved to her new apartment. She looks much **happier** now.

If the adjective is three syllables long and ends in *y*, change *y* to *ier*, or use the *more...than* form of comparison.

lovely, **lovelier** OR **more lovely than**
lonely, **lonelier** OR **more lonely than**
Jasmin looks **lovelier** without make-up.
Jasmin looks **more lovely** without make-up.

She felt even **lonelier** after her transfer.
She felt even **more lonely** after her transfer.

LONGER ADJECTIVES

For longer adjectives, use the *more...than* form.

beautiful, **more beautiful than**
intelligent, **more intelligent than**
expensive, **more expensive than**
This coat is **more expensive than** that one.
His cousin is **more intelligent than** he is.

TWO-SYLLABLE ADJECTIVES

Some two-syllable adjectives can take either the *r/er* form or the *more...than* form.

clever, **cleverer** OR **more clever than**
simple, **simpler** OR **more simple than**

Other examples are *unkind, narrow, common, quiet.*

This dress pattern is **simpler than** that one.
This dress pattern is **more simple** than that one.

*Your plan seems **cleverer than** your partner's.*
*Your plan seems **more clever than** your partner's.*

IRREGULAR ADJECTIVES

a) Three very common adjectives have irregular comparative forms.
    *good, **better***
    *bad, **worse***
    *far, **farther***
    *Blue looks **better** on you than yellow.*
    *Johnny wrote **a worse** composition than his sister.*
    *Niagara Falls is **farther** from Toronto **than** from Burlington.*

b) **Older** and **elde**r are used in different ways. *Older* is used for comparison.
    *My father is six months **older than** his brother, Sacha.*

    Elder is an old form, mainly used in phrases such as an *elder sister, elder brother, elder son. Elder* is never used comparatively with *than.*

12.2 THE COMPARATIVE OF ADVERBS

REGULAR ADVERBS

In general, adverbs follow the same rules as adjectives to form the comparative.
    *soon, **sooner***
    *late, **later***
    *near, **nearer***
    *He came **sooner than** I expected.*
    *This morning, I got to class **later than** usual.*

However, for adverbs of two or more syllables ending in *ly*, the rule is different. For these adverbs, use the *more...than* form.
    *slowly, **more slowly***
    *intelligently, **more intelligently***
    *Please drive **more slowly**.*
    *He speaks **more intelligently** than his friend.*

well, **better**   *far,* **farther**
badly, **worse**   *little,* **less**
He works **better** *than his brother does.*
She ran **farther** *than her sister did.*

12.3 THE COMPARATIVE OF NOUNS

More + **Noun** + *than* is used to form the comparative of a noun.
There are **more** *foreign films on Channel 14* **than** *on Channel 19.*
They bought **more** *apples* **than** *oranges for the picnic.*

12.4 COMPARING PRECISELY

An expression of measure, quantity or amount may precede the comparative form. Its function is to indicate the exact difference between the two items being compared.
She is **five centimetres taller than** *her brother.*
Paul is **two years older than** *Susan.*
She gave me **$10 more than** *I charged her.*
There were at least **15 people fewer than** *we expected.*

12.5 COMPARISON OF EQUALITY

AS...AS

When two items are equal in size, shape, weight or quantity, use *as...as* with the adjective or adverb.
Is Lucy **as tall as** *her mother?*
She didn't do the work **as well as** *I expected.*
The work wasn't **as hard as** *I first thought.*

THE SAME AS

The same means identical. It is used with or without a noun and can be followed by an *as* expression of comparison.

> *My mother's hat is the same colour **as** yours.*
> *Our apartments are **the same** size.*
> *He expressed **the same interest as** many others.*

Note: The opposite of *the same* is **different (from)**.

> *The layout of my apartment is **different from** yours.*
> *Our sofas are **different**.*

12.6 INTENSIFIERS WITH COMPARISONS

Intensifiers such as *almost, practically* and *just* can be used with *as...as*.

> *This suit is **just as elegant** as that one.*
> *Their project is **practically as complicated as** ours.*
> *That young actor performs **almost as naturally as** an actor with more experience.*

Much, many, a lot, a little and *a bit* can also be used as modifiers before adjectives.

> *John is a **much better** swimmer than Mia.*
> *Ellen is **a lot more personable** than her cousin.*
> *I'm feeling **a little better** today, thank you.*

12.7 CORRELATION

Two clauses or phrases with **the** + Adjective or Adverb in the comparative can be used to express **correlation**.

> *The **harder** I work, **the happier** I am.*
> *The **more** they study, **the better** they become.*

The subject and verb of the second clause may be dropped if the meaning is obvious.

> *The **less** candy you eat, **the better**.*
> *What time shall we have lunch?*
> *The **later**, **the better** for me.*

12.8 THE SUPERLATIVE FORM OF ADJECTIVES

The **superlative form** is used to compare more than two items in size, weight, shape, age, quantity or quality.

The preposition *in* is used before the group or area in which the comparison is made, and, if necessary, *of* is used before the items compared.

> *This old Rolls Royce is the most expensive **of** all the cars **in** the museum.*
> *The Nile is **the longest river** in the world.*

The superlative form of adjectives is always preceded by *the* or *a*.

SHORT ADJECTIVES OF ONE SYLLABLE

If the adjective ends in *e*, add *st*.
> *large, **the largest***
> *gentle, **the gentlest***
> *wise, **the wisest***
> *Our kitchen is **the largest** room in the house.*
> *My grandmother is **the wisest** in the family.*

If the adjective does not end in *e*, add *est*.
> *young, **the youngest***
> *new, **the newest***
> *small, **the smallest***
> *Sarah is **the youngest** student of all.*
> *My red sweater is **my newest** sweater.*

If the adjective ends in one consonant, double the consonant and add *est*.
> *cold, **the coldest***
> *hot, **the hottest***
> *fast, **the fastest***
> *It has been **the hottest** summer in 15 years.*
> *In my country, June and July are **the coldest** months.*

ADJECTIVES ENDING IN Y
If the adjective ends in *y*, change *y* to *iest*.
> *sunny, **the sunniest***

pretty, **the prettiest**
busy, **the busiest**
College Boulevard is **the busiest** *street in the neighbourhood.*
I just bought **the prettiest** *flower arrangement of all.*

You can also use **the most** + Adjective form.
lovely, **the most lovely**
wealthy, **the most wealthy**
Heidi wore **her most lovely** *dress.*
Uncle Karl is **the most wealthy** *man in the family.*

LONG ADJECTIVES

For longer adjectives, use *the most* + adjective form.
beautiful, **the most beautiful**
expensive, **the most expensive**
intelligent, **the most intelligent**
She bought **the most expensive** *saxophone in the store.*
Maria is **the most intelligent** *student of all in my class.*

TWO-SYLLABLE ADJECTIVES

Some two-syllable adjectives can take either *the...st/est* or *the most* form.
clever, **the cleverest** *OR* **the most clever**
simple, **the simplest** *OR* **the most simple**

Other examples are *common, narrow, quiet* and *handsome.*
She is the **quietest/most quiet** *student in class.*
This is the **commonest/most common** *mistake.*

IRREGULAR ADJECTIVES

The three common adjectives that have irregular comparative forms,
also have irregular forms in the superlative.
good, **the best**
bad, **the worst**
far, **the farthest**
Oliver's Bakery sells **the best** *garlic bread in town.*
Of all my co-workers, I live **the farthest.**
I'm **the worst** *cook in my family.*

12.9 THE SUPERLATIVE OF ADVERBS

REGULAR ADVERBS

In general, adverbs follow the same rule as adjectives to form the superlative.

*soon, **the soonest***
*late, **the latest***
*near, **the nearest***
*Of all the students, Alfredo arrives **the latest**.*
*My youngest brother lives **the nearest** to me.*

However, for adverbs of two or more syllables ending in *ly*, the rule is different. *The most* precedes them.

*slowly, **the most slowly***
*intelligent, **the most intelligently***
*Huong drove **the most slowly** of all the drivers.*
*Rebecca acted **the most intelligently**.*

IRREGULAR ADVERBS

Several adverbs have an irregular form in the superlative.

*well, **the best***
*badly, **the worst***
*little, **the least***
*far, **the farthest***
*Of all the speakers, Mr. Chen spoke **the best** and Mr. Mandoza **the least**.*

12.10 COMPARATIVE AND SUPERLATIVE OF INFERIORITY

To indicate inferiority in scale, degree or quantity, **less** is used for the comparative and **the least** for the superlative. *Less* and the *least* are placed before the adverb or the adjective.

*beautiful, **less beautiful**, **the least beautiful***
*noisy, **less noisy**, **the least noisy***

*Our new neighbours are **less noisy** than our old ones were.*
*We bought **the least** expensive house.*

12.11 COMPARATIVE AND SUPERLATIVE OF QUANTIFIERS

Much, many, and *little* have irregular comparative and superlative forms.
   much, ***more, the most***
   many, ***more, the most***
   little, ***less, the least***
   I weigh ***more*** than Mary.
   The Browns gave ***the most*** to the Cancer Society.

12.12 EXERCISES

IMPROVE YOUR SPEAKING AND WRITING

1.   Complete the following sentences with the comparative of the italicized noun. (See 12.3.)

EXAMPLE: I need **more** *hours of sleep* than most of my classmates.

   a)   The taxi driver asked for _____ *directions* because he wasn't familiar with the neighbourhood.

   b)   The swimmers won _____ *medals* _____ other athletes in the last national competition.

   c)   The injured tennis player is going to need _____ *hours of physiotherapy* before he can compete again.

   d)   Food banks are going to call for _____ donations soon.

   e)   The school next door is going to hire _____ *part-time teachers* _____ full-time ones next year.

   f)   The car dealership in our district sold _____ *used cars* _____ new ones last year.

   g)   The woman with the grey fur hat always buys _____ *lottery tickets* _____ her white-haired companion.

h) The Federal government promised _____ *education funds* for the coming year.

i) The real estate agent is going to send _____ *publicity brochures* in the hope of attracting _____ buyers.

j) The young travellers ate _____ *sandwiches* _____ anything else during their tour of Australia.

k) The aggressive sales representative received a special bonus at Christmas because she had sold _____ *encyclopedias* _____ any other employee in the firm.

l) The steelworker took _____ *days off* _____ his fellow workers.

m) Gardeners now use _____ *organic materials* _____ before.

2. Work with a partner. Compare the following pairs of items in two sentences. Use *much* or *a little* when possible. (See 12.1.)

EXAMPLE: gold/silver (expensive)

Gold is more expensive.

Gold is much more expensive than silver.

a) a van/a Honda (big)

b) a horror movie/a detective movie (frightening)

c) Greece/England (warm)

d) Saskatchewan's climate/England's climate (dry)

e) fibre-rich cereals/creamy pastries (healthy)

f) a dancer/a weight lifter (thin)

g) Southern Ontario soil/Northern Ontario soil (fertile)

h) a precious stone/a synthetic stone (prized)

i) fresh-cut flowers/plastic flowers (beautiful)

j) a kitten/an old cat (playful)

k) nightingales/owls (musical)

l) fine French lace/Swiss eyelet (delicate)

m) a steep mountain/a rolling hill (impressive)

n) sulphur/rubbing alcohol (smelly)

o) jogging/walking (strenuous)

p) a cup of chicken broth/a cup of coffee (nutritious)

q) a corner variety store/a delicatessen (convenient)

r) pneumonia/a regular cold (dangerous)

s) a basketball player/a jockey (tall)

t) spring water/tap water (pure)

3. Compare the following pairs. You and a partner can take turns.

EXAMPLE:

Vishal, 15 years old, 165 cm tall, 65 kg	Yvan, 17 years old, 170 cm tall, 60 kg

Vishal is two years younger than Yvan, 5 cm shorter and 5 kg heavier (OR weighs 5 kg more).

Yvan is two years older than Vishal, 5 cm taller and 5 kg lighter (OR weighs 5 kg less).

a)

Mary Ann, 28 years old, 60 kg, 172 cm tall	Nina, 20 years old, 52 kg, 170 cm tall

b)

Tom works 50 hours a week, sleeps 7 hours every night, exercises twice a week.	Dino works 40 hours a week, sleeps 8 hours every night, exercises once a week.

c)

Sonia has three pets, nine plants and two guitars in her house.	Maria has two pets, five plants and one guitar in her house.

d)

| A cashmere sweater, long-sleeved, warm, royal blue, expensive | A cotton sweater, short-sleeved, cool, powder blue, inexpensive |

4. Work with a partner. Make two statements, each giving a precise comparison.

EXAMPLE: The living room ceiling is 3 m high.

The hallway ceiling is 5 m high.

The hallway ceiling is **2 m higher** than the living room ceiling.

The living room ceiling is **2 m lower** than the hallway ceiling.

a)   Dahlia is 15 years old. Natasha is 17 years old.

b)   Benjamin stands 180 cm tall. Tamara 155 cm.

c)   The football coach cancelled two practice sessions this season. The soccer coach cancelled five.

d)   The newspaper editor made $40,000 last year. This year $50,000.

e)   Larry is going to order 900 L (litres) of fuel. Nick, 600 L.

f)   The Swiss mountain climbers climbed 100 m. The French, 250 m.

g)   The orange wire seems to be about one metre long. The blue one about two metres.

h)   Sutton Contractors are going to dredge three river beds. The Dreiser Company, nine.

i)   The suit made in Canada costs $800. The one made in Japan, $400.

j)   The conference room looks 3 m wide. The boardroom looks 4 m wide.

k)   The red-brick townhouses are five years old. The yellow townhouses, eight years old.

l)   The emergency ward doctor examined 50 patients yesterday. The general practitioner examined 20.

m)   At the science contest, the first examiner gave the best entry 10 points. The second one, eight.

n) I am going to visit five pavilions at the Epcot Centre. My companions, seven.

o) Detective Simon is investigating six robbery cases. Sergeant Weir, two.

p) The ferry ride to the Toronto Islands is 10 minutes long. The cruise on the Chief Commanda in North Bay is 75 minutes long.

q) Frank skipped one class yesterday. Raymond, two.

5. Complete the following sentences with the superlative form of the adjective or adverb provided. (See 12.8 and 12.9.)

EXAMPLE: I would like to go to Spadina Avenue. Which is **the shortest** (short) way?

a) There were five questions on the test. I started with _____ (easy) one.

b) We saw 10 beautiful loveseats. We chose _____ (comfortable) one.

c) Do you want to go downtown? It is _____ (lively) area in this city.

d) All the customers left the restaurant happy. Zelda tipped the waiter _____ (generously).

e) There was a mountain of mangoes on the stand. People selected _____ (ripe) ones.

f) Do you need some peace and quiet? The office on the second floor is _____ (quiet) place in the building.

g) We want Milan Noli on our team! He is _____ (good) player in the school!

h) The clerk showed me half a dozen winter parkas. I bought _____ (warm) one.

i) This artist is going to exhibit her work in a small gallery. Do you want to see her _____ (late) paintings?

j) I am not surprised that they are doing so well in business. They only carry _____ (marketable) products.

k) Carol Betts has a green thumb. She grows _____ (healthy) and

_____ (beautiful) roses in the neighbourhood.

l)   You love fish and chips? I know where they make _____ (good) ones in town.

m)   That store sells a great variety of coffees. We usually buy _____ (strong) one.

n)   I want to buy a good English dictionary. Which is _____ (good)?

o)   The Smith brothers are coming to Toronto next week. I only know _____ (young) one.

p)   We need quite a few things for our new home. We will start with the _____ (necessary) ones.

q)   The travel agency was advertising many trips. I looked for _____ (exciting) one.

6.   Complete the following sentences with the comparative or the superlative form of the adverb.

EXAMPLE: A: Tara speaks English fluently.

B: Does she speak English **more fluently than** Claire?

a)   A: My brother visits my parents frequently.
     B: Does he visit them _____ you?

b)   A: Chemists treat the pollution issue seriously.
     B: True, but they don't treat it any _____ biologists.

c)   A: Did it rain heavily on Monday?
     B: Yes, but it rained _____ today.

d)   A: We all applauded enthusiastically.
     B: I applauded _____ of all because my daughter had the lead part.

e)   A: Tom has always shopped wisely.
     B: Now, because he has no job, he shops _____ ever.

f)   A: The pilot spoke competently about air safety.
     B: Did he speak _____ the flight attendant?

g) A: Many of the guests are coming from far away.

   B: Ron is going to drive _____ of all. He lives 200 km away.

h) A: Olga's brothers live close to her.

   B: Yes, and her youngest brother lives _____ . His house is one block down the street.

i) A: Does Tofa arrive at school early?

   B: Yes, she sometimes arrives even _____ the teacher.

j) A: The two friends are nervous about their TOEFL.

   B: Toban is _____ than Steven because he needs a high score for university.

k) A: The ballet students of the Light Slipper dance school often win in competitions.

   B: Yes, indeed. And Tanya Beder has won _____ awards of all.

l) A: My relatives in Japan gave a lot to the Youth Foundation.

   B: Katsumi Nakasone contributed _____ . She is usually quite generous.

m) A: People were late today because of the fog.

   B: I also got to work _____ usual this morning.

n) A: The janitors in my building are working long hours this week.

   B: Patricia is working _____ of all.

o) A: The Grade six students were very excited about Hallowe'en.

   B: Norma was _____ of all because she was going to be the wicked witch in the play.

p) A: All the students in my art class paint beautifully.

   B: Lorenzo paints by far _____ of all.

q) A: Is your uncle from Europe coming to visit you soon?

   B: He is coming _____ expected.

r) A. The bird-watchers were walking slowly.

   B: Dragy was walking _____ the others because of an injured knee.

7. Combine each pair of sentences into one sentence by using the comparative of equality. (See 12.5.)

EXAMPLE: The Kucharski's yacht is 15 m long.

So is the Neilson's.

The Kucharski's yacht is as long as the Neilson's.

a) Computer programming is difficult. So is mathematics.

b) This businessperson looks wise. So does her partner.

c) The first composition topic is interesting. So is the third.

d) Alain drives carefully. So does his brother.

e) Sara has many chores at home. So does Gustavo.

f) The cotton dress dried quickly. So did the silk shirt.

g) Walking briskly is good for the circulation. So is swimming.

h) Chandran's objections caused little surprise at the meeting. So did Clara's.

i) The male voices in the choir were warm and clear. So were the female voices.

j) The English consultant is teaching two hours a day. So is our ESL department head.

k) The international champions are going to compete tomorrow. So are the national ones.

l) The sunroom on the magazine's front cover is very inviting. So is the garden on its back cover.

8. Reword the following sentences by using the comparative of inferiority. (See 12.10.)

EXAMPLE: The video cassette recorder is not as useful to me as the portable cassette player.

The video cassette recorder is less useful to me than the portable cassette player.

a) The new employee at Sandy's isn't as experienced as I thought.

b) Last night was not so foggy as tonight.

c) February was not as productive as March.

d) This roast does not look as lean as the one I bought at Bruno's.

e) Parisa did not complain about the long hours as loudly as Danilo.

f) There was not as much tension in this meeting as in the previous one.

g) The older applicants did not seem so interested in working overtime as the younger ones.

h) The general manager of this store is not as powerful as he presents himself to be.

i) Ramona's new line of accessories is not as popular as her last one.

j) Some people are not as keen on fighting pollution as they should be.

k) Tony didn't react as coldly as his sister when I asked them for a loan.

l) The young storyteller does not catch the audience's imagination as quickly as the old master.

m) Kindergarten children do not cry as much on the second day as they do on the first.

n) Our Grade Twelve students aren't as creative as our Grade Eleven students.

9. Express the adjectives provided in the comparative form, and then complete the sentences with one of the following intensifiers: *almost, even, practically, just, a lot, a little, a bit.* Use more than one intensifier where possible.

EXAMPLE: A: Is this coat as elegant as my favourite green one?

B: Definitely. This coat is **even more elegant** (elegant).

a) A: Is Susan still taking dancing lessons?

B: She certainly is. And I find she is _____ (good) _____ last year!

b) A: Did you watch J. Toro's latest documentary?

B: Yes, it was _____ (interesting) _____ her last one.

c) A: Did Charles make his speech last Tuesday?

B: He did, and his speech was _____ (convincing) _____ Tara's.

d) A: Do you have another solution to this problem?

B: Yes, I do. My solution is _____ (practical) _____ yours. Let me explain why.

e) A: Did you read yesterday's editorial in the Herald?

B: Yes. That editorial was _____ (critical) of the situation _____ last week's.

f) A: Are we taking the highway?

B: Yes, we are. After its last tune-up, my car is _____ (reliable) _____ it used to be.

g) A: Which do you find more useful? A computer or a typewriter?

B: A computer is _____ (useful). It performs so many extra functions.

h) A: Do you have any pain in your back now?

B: Yes, I do. As a matter of fact, I am feeling _____ (bad) today.

i) A: How did you find the grammar exam?

B: It was _____ (difficult) _____ I expected.

10. Comment on the pairs of sentences by using the comparative form. (See 12.7.)

EXAMPLE: I am busy. I am happy.

The busier I am, the happier I am.

a) You read a lot. You learn a lot.

b) You earn a lot. You pay a lot of income tax.

c) The athlete exercises a lot. He feels good.

d) I know Tom well. I like him.

e) You practice a lot. Your pronunciation improves a lot.

f) I'm very busy. I see a few of my friends.

g) You worry a lot. You feel a lot of tension.

h) The ambitious landlord renovated a lot. He increased the rent a lot.

i) The insurance broker's car got old. She spent a lot on repairs.

j) The bricklayers are going to start work earlier. They are going to accomplish a lot in a day.

k) We water the grass regularly. It grows well.

l) You have a lot of experience. You work fast.

11. Work with a partner. Take turns reading each pair of sentences, then combining them with a comparative form.

EXAMPLE: Our paper boy delivers a hundred papers. So does his sister.

Our paper boy delivers the same number of papers as his sister.

a) Tony travels 15 km to go to work every day. So does his wife.

b) Let's order sole fillet with vegetables. That's what we had last time.

c) My cousin is 23 years old. So is his girlfriend.

d) The chef at the Caledonia Inn enjoys playing chess. So does the sous-chef.

e) The economics major is taking a math course. So is the math major.

f) The Italian group of experts visited a Swiss watch manufacturing company. So did the French delegation.

g) Ovide speaks Cree. So does Jack.

h) Many T.V. personalities are going to join the food drive. So are their radio colleagues.

i) My mother takes seven pills a day. So does my grandmother.

j) Shushana takes guitar lessons on Monday and Wednesday nights. So does her best friend.

k) The Tudor-style bungalow costs $400,000. So does the Victorian-style side-split house.

l) Peter is going to celebrate his graduation on Saturday June 5th. So are his classmates.

m) The grocer in the small plaza lost $60,000 last year. So did the butcher.

EXPRESS YOURSELF

1. Answer the following questions using the comparative form. You may use your own words or the words provided.

EXAMPLE: Why do people travel by train? (comfortable)

People travel by train because it is more comfortable. But the train is more expensive than the bus.

   a) Why do many Canadians spend the winter in Florida? (warm)
   b) Why do people eat at home rather than eat out? (economical)
   c) Why are some businesses registering lower profits? (few sales)
   d) Why do people use bank machines? (fast)
   e) Why do people take courses in English as a Second Language? (speak well)
   f) How is your English now compared to a few months ago? (fluent)
   g) Why do students study in the library? (quiet/resources)
   h) Why do people buy expensive appliances? (dependable)
   i) Why do people wallpaper their homes? (look attractive)
   j) Why do people trim their hedges? (look neat)
   k) Why do people work overtime? (a lot of money)
   l) Why do tourists love the Canadian West so much? (beautiful)
   m) Why do nutritionists recommend vegetables in our diet? (nutritious)
   n) Why do some children prefer rice pudding to plain rice? (sweet)
   o) How do people feel after surgery? (weak)
   p) How do people feel during a holiday? (rested)

2. Make complete questions using your own words and the suggested words. Then interview your partner. Your partner will answer in complete statements.

EXAMPLE: (Who is/active/your class)

Who is the most active student in your class?

Luba is the most active student in my class. She works the longest hours.

   a) (Who is/tall/your family)

b) (Who cooks/delicious/meals/your family)

c) (When did you have to make/hard/decision/your life)

d) (What personal achievement are you/proud of)

e) (What do you consider your/prized/possession)

f) (Who is/good/friend)

g) (What activities or hobbies/enjoy/most)

h) (What do you find/irritating/thing/in life)

i) (What do you find/rewarding/thing/in life)

j) (Which English sounds are/difficult/for you)

k) (When you went to school, what was your/good/subject)

l) (When you went to school, what was your/bad/subject)

m) (Who's got/rich/vocabulary/your class)

n) (Who has/challenging/job/among your acquaintances)

o) (Which is/boring/program/on television)

p) (Which is/interesting/program/on television)

q) (Who are/important/political figures/the world)

r) (What is/great threat/to the environment)

3. Work with a partner and compare yourselves.

a) Who speaks more English outside of class?

b) Who writes more letters to friends?

c) Who likes travelling more?

d) Who reads more English books?

e) Who wears a larger size of clothes?

f) Who practices more sports?

g) Who is more interested in politics?

h) Who watches more T.V.?

i) Who spends more time cooking?

j) Who lives closer to the school?

4. Compare your country of origin to this country. Consider the cost of housing, the working hours, the kinds of food, and the forms of

entertainment. Work with a partner first. Then write a paragraph with the comparisons.

5. Work with a partner. Ask your partner the following questions. Your partner will answer in complete statements.

a) Which are the most industrialized countries in the world?

b) Which countries are the largest producers of grain? Oil?

c) Which is the largest country in the world?

d) Which is the second largest country in the world?

e) Which is the largest continent in the world?

f) Which is the largest island in the world?

g) Which is the largest lake in Canada?

h) Which is the longest river in Canada?

i) Which is the tallest mountain in Canada?

j) Which is the largest province in Canada?

k) Which is the smallest province in Canada?

l) How can one travel the most economically in this country?

6. Work with a partner. Discuss the following topics. Then write a paragraph about what you discussed.

a) You need a new television set. You've seen two sets that you like very much. Compare these two sets in terms of size, weight, price, warranty, quality of the picture, quality of the sound.

b) You need a coat. You've seen two that you like. Compare them in terms of colour, style, price, material.

7. Work with a partner. Ask your partner the following questions. Your partner will answer in complete statements and will explain his or her answers. Them write down the information.

a) What do you think is the most interesting way of spending a holiday?

b) Which is the most enjoyable sport to you?

c) Who are the most important people in your life?

d) What is the main goal in your life?

e) What is your most pleasant memory?

f) What activity do you find most relaxing?

8. Tell a partner, then write about the following:

   a) The most disappointing news you've ever heard

   b) The most exciting news you've ever heard

9. Work with a partner. Find out about your partner's lifestyle. Ask your partner questions about
   - home
   - family
   - hobbies

   Then write a short paragraph comparing your lifestyle to your partner's. Write at least two sentences on each of the topics above.

EXAMPLE: **My place is smaller but brighter than my friend's. My rent is higher.**

UNIT 13 – CONCEPTS WITH MODALS

13.1 MODALS IN GENERAL

INTRODUCTION

Modals are helping verbs. They are used with the main verb in a sentence to indicate a mood, a concept or a certain precise idea. As this unit will explain, modals help express a variety of meanings.

The best way to master modals is to understand the different meanings of each one, to learn when and how to use modals, and to practice them in sentences.

Some modals are *can, could, may, might, shall, should, will, would, must, ought to* and *have to*.

GENERAL RULES

a) A modal is always used with the main verb in the infinitive. The main verb can be omitted if it has already been mentioned in an earlier context.
    Can she *drive* a car? Sure, she *can*.

b) Modals do not have *s* forms (except *have to*).
    She *has* to go.

c) Some past forms of modals are also used to express present or future time.
    He *might* leave tomorrow.   He *might* leave now.

d) A modal that is used to express present time can also express future time with the addition of a future time expression.
    I *can* finish the work now. I *can* finish the work *tomorrow*.

e) Most modals form contractions with *not*.
    cannot, can't   could not, couldn't
    might not, mightn't   should not, shouldn't
    will not, won't   would not, wouldn't
    must not, mustn't.

Note: *May* and *ought to* do not form contractions. *Have to* follows the rules for the verb *have* in forming negative and interrogative forms.
     She **doesn't have** to work this weekend.
     Does she **have** to work this weekend?

f) To form questions, modals are usually placed before the subject.
*Can you **play** the piano?*

g) Negative modals do not always express the opposite of their affirmative forms.
must = *obligation*
mustn't = *prohibition*

h) A modal can express more than one concept.
may = *permission*
may = *probability*

13.2 PERMISSION

IN THE PRESENT

a) **May** is used for asking and giving permission.
May I have some candy?
Yes, you may.

May I leave early?
*No, you **may** not.*
*You **may** let the cat in now.*

b) In conversational style, **can** or **could** is often used instead of may.
Can I watch T.V. tonight?
*No, you **can't**.*

Could I use your phone?
Of course.

Can't is used in the sense of "not allowed or permitted to."
*I'm sorry, but you **can't** park your motorbike here.*

IN THE PAST

a) **May**, meaning permission, is not used in the past. This idea is expressed with **have permission** to or **be allowed to**.
*I **had permission** to leave at 3:00.*
*We **weren't allowed** to use the computer after school.*

b) **Could** expresses permission in the past. It means "was/were allowed to."
*The security guard **could** smoke only in the staff room on her breaks.*

c) If the activity was allowed and performed, **was/were allowed to** are usually used.
*Each girl **was allowed to** have a dessert of her choice. Janet chose chocolate cake.*

13.3 FUTURE

There are many ways of expressing future time.

WITH THE APPROPRIATE TENSE

a) **Be going to**, as explained in Unit 9, indicates intention, a premeditated future.
*This Sunday, we **are going to** drive to the country and have a picnic. (We have planned to do this.)*

b) The **present continuous tense** is used for a definite plan in the near future.
We're driving *to the cottage this afternoon.*

c) The **simple present tense** is used for a planned future action, or series of actions, referring to a schedule, a timetable or travel.
*Class **begins** at 9:00 next Monday.*
*The plane **leaves** at 4:10 sharp on Tuesday afternoon.*

d) The **simple present tense** is also usually used with verbs of motion such as *come, go, leave,* and *arrive* and, with a word indicating future time to express a future action.
*We **leave** for New York tomorrow afternoon.*
*Next week, he **goes** to Calgary and Vancouver.*

WITH THE MODAL WILL

a) **Will** expresses future intention. But unlike with *be going to*, this intention is unpremeditated.

*I bought a new cassette. I'm **going to** listen to it this afternoon. (premeditated)*
*There's no more butter? I'**ll** buy some tomorrow. (unpremeditated)*
Sometimes either **be going to** or will can be used.
*I will visit my family in Somalia next year. **I am going to** visit my family in Somalia next year.*

b)   *Will* also indicates some willingness or determination in the future.
*The phone is ringing! I'**ll** get it!*

c)   *Will* expresses promise.
*I **will** call you as soon as your order comes in.*

d)   *Will* expresses a certain degree of prediction.
*The sky is cloudy. It **will** rain tomorrow.*

Will be + the *ing* form of the verb expresses ongoing action at a certain time in the future.
*Don't call her at noon, she'**ll be feeding** her baby.*
*At this time tomorrow, I'**ll be lying** on the beach.*

e)   *Will not* (won't) indicates refusal.
*His father **won't** let him drive at night.*
*I **won't** put up with that noise! Turn off the radio!*

WITH THE EXPRESSION *BE ABOUT TO*

Be about to + simple form of verb expresses the immediate future.
*The meeting **is about to start**. (The meeting is going to start now.)*
*They're **just about to leave**. (**Just** emphasizes the nearness of a future event.)*

13.4   NECESSITY AND OBLIGATION

Must**, **have to** and **should express the idea of necessity and obligation.
a)   ***Must*** is used to state a general truth, a rule or a regulation. It also indicates a strong sense of duty or moral obligation.
*Plumbers **must** have a licence to work in Canada.*
*You **must** obey the law.*

*Parents **must** listen to their children.*

b) ***Must*** and ***have to*** are used to express necessity. They indicate a course of action that we think necessary.
*I **must/have to** leave now.*
*He **must/has** to fly to Winnipeg next week.*
*I can't watch T.V. now. I **have to** do my homework.*

Note: When *must* means necessity, it does not have a past form. Necessity in the past is expressed with *had to*.

*He **had to** work overtime to pay for his new car.*

c) ***Don't have to*** in the present and ***didn't have to*** in the past express the absence of necessity.
*His parents are well off. He **doesn't have to** work.*
*His parents were well off. He **didn't have to** work.*

Note: In making questions, the have to forms are usually used for necessity.

*Do you **have to** work late again tonight?*
*Did you **have to** tell them the truth?*

d) *Be to* + simple form of verb expresses duty or obligation. It also indicates an arrangement, a plan or an agreement as the result of a decision, a request or a command.
*No one **is to leave** the room without permission. (The teacher said so.)*
*The Prime Minister **is to visit** Japan soon. (This visit has been arranged.)*

13.5 RECOMMENDATION AND ADVICE

a) ***Should*** is generally used when giving and asking advice.
*You **shouldn't** smoke so much!*
*What **should** I do to get rid of these stains?*

Like *must* and *have to*, *should* is used for present or future time.
*I **shouldn't** drink so much coffee. (every day)*
*We **should** visit her soon. (in the future)*

Should be + present participle expresses obligation, recommendation or advice in the present time (now).

*You **shouldn't be playing** tennis now. You **should be studying** for your exams.*

b) ***Ought to*** and ***should*** both express moral obligation, but *ought to* is rarely used.

*We really **ought** to visit her more often.*
*We **should** help the poor.*

c) ***Had better*** *('d better)* also expresses advisability, and always indicates present or future time. It has no past. The negative form is *had better not ('d better not).*

*We'**d better** hurry if we want to be on time.*
*You'**d better** not be late again or else I'll report you to the office.*
*They'**d better** not tell her what happened. Otherwise, she'll be very upset!*

Note: *Had better* is not used in questions; use *should* instead.

***Should** we leave now or wait until Mehdi can drive us home?*
***Shouldn't** she get some rest before her exam?*

d) ***Might***, ***could*** and ***why don't you*** can also express recommendation and advice.

*If you want to meet new people, you **might** join a social club.*
*If you don't enjoy gardening, you **could** hire a student to cut the grass.*
***Why don't you** wear gardening gloves? You're ruining your hands.*

13.6 PROBABILITY, LIKELIHOOD AND POSSIBILITY

a) ***Must*** is a deductive modal that expresses some certainty about an event. It is used to indicate deduction, a strong probability or likelihood.

*Their children are successful. They **must** be very proud of them.*
*She lived in France for quite a long time. She **must** speak French well.*

b) ***It is likely*** and the adverb ***probably*** can also express probability or likelihood.

*It is **likely*** that he'll invite them to the party.
He **probably** went out of town for the weekend.

Unlikelihood is expressed with **it is unlikely**.
It is unlikely that he'll invite them to the party.

c) **Should** can also indicate probability or expectancy.
*Where's George? He **should** be in his room. (I think he's there.)*
*Her poem is beautiful. It **should** win first prize. (I expect her poem to win. It is very likely that it will win.)*

d) **May** and **might** express a more remote possibility or probability.
*He **may (might)** move to a larger apartment. (Maybe he'll move to a larger apartment. It is possible that he'll move.)*

> **Note:** *May, might, must* and *should* are not used in the interrogative to express possibility or probability. Expressions such as *Do you think* or *Do you know* are used instead.

Do you think *they are proud of their children?*
Do you know *where George is?*

f) **Can't** expresses impossibility, a negative deduction.
*She **can't be** in her office. I just talked to her at home. (It is impossible that she is in her office.)*
*She **may not be in her office**, on the other hand, means that it is possible she is not in her office.*

13.7 ABILITY

Can and **be able to** express the idea of ability in present time. However, *can* is more common.
>*He **can** type 70 words a minute.*
>***Can*** *you sing?*

Could and **was/were able to** express past ability.
>*At 10, he **could/was able to** swim across the river.*

However, *was/were able to* is used to express the combined idea of ability and the success of a particular action.
>*In two years, they **were able to** save enough money to buy a car.*

*After he tried a few times, he **was able to** unlock the door.*

To express the negative, use **can't** or **be not able to** in the present, and **couldn't** or **was/were not able to** in the past.

*I **can't** ski.*

*She **is not able to** do math very well.*

*A few months ago, I **couldn't** speak English at all.*

*Even after two years, they **weren't able to** buy a car.*

13.8 PROHIBITION

a) **Mustn't** is used to express prohibition. The *not* makes the verb following the modal negative.

*She **mustn't** eat dairy products. (She is forbidden to eat dairy products.)*

b) **Can't** and **may not** also express prohibition. They mean "not allowed/permitted to."

*You **can't** take these books home. The sign says, "Do not remove." (You are not allowed to take these books home.)*

c) The **be not to + simple form of verb** also indicates prohibition.

*You **are not to leave** the room without permission.*

13.9 OFFER OF SERVICE AND REQUESTS

a) **Shall I** introduces an offer of service.

***Shall I** put the wine glasses away? (Do you want me to put them away?)*

*Are you hungry? **Shall I** make you a sandwich?*

A polite request can be introduced with expressions such as the following:

***Could** you please help me with this exercise?*

***Would** you tell Mr. Singh that I called?*

***Please** open the door for me.*

An informal request can be introduced with expressions such as these:

Can you give me a ride to the subway?
Will you give her my message?

13.10 PREFERENCE

Would rather expresses preference in the present or future time. *Than* can be used to indicate the standard against which the preference is made.

*Dilip **would rather** watch T.V. than study. (now)*
*Lucy **would rather** go for a walk. (this afternoon)*
Would you like a coffee?
*I'**d rather** have something cold, if you don't mind.*

In the interrogative, the subject is placed between *would* and *rather.*

*Would **you** rather go for a walk or swim?*
*Would **she** rather play football or hockey?*

The negative is expressed with *not.*

*I would rather **not** talk to him now.*

Would rather can be contracted to *'d rather* with pronouns in conversation.

*I'**d rather** stay home than go out with him.*
*She'**d rather** not speak to him now.*

13.11 EXERCISES

IMPROVE YOUR SPEAKING AND WRITING

1. Complete the following sentences with the verb provided to express future time with *will*. Use the contracted forms when possible.

EXAMPLE: *Will* all stores open on Boxing Day?

No, they **won't**.

a)   The new library _____ (open) this spring.

b)   _____ the newspaper _____ (cover) the International Horse Show?

265

c) _____ you _____ (come) to my party if I invite you?

d) The doctor _____ (see) you without an appointment.

e) I am sure these young people _____ (succeed) in life.

f) Wait for me in front of the drugstore. I _____ (pick you up) at four.

g) Don't worry! I _____ (look after) the bill!

h) Where _____ you _____ (live)?
   I _____ (live) with my aunt for a few months, then I _____ (look for) an apartment.

i) My sister is going to Italy for a year!
   That _____ (be) quite an experience for her.

j) What are their plans?
   They _____ (run away from home) and _____ (get) married in Las Vegas.

k) What time _____ you _____ (be) back?
   I _____ (be) back in just an hour.

l) Don't worry! I _____ (say) anything to anybody.

m) Now that Michael is on a diet, he _____ (eat) any sweets or fatty foods.

n) When _____ they _____ (finish) the bridge?
   They _____ (finish) it in a couple of months.

2. What are these people saying? Follow the example.

EXAMPLE:

A: What will you do next summer?

B: I will go camping.

a) A: _____ tomorrow?

266

B: _____

_____

b) A: _____ next Saturday?

B: _____

_____

c) A: _____ in two days?

B: _____

_____

d) A: _____ tonight?

B: _____

_____

e) A: _____ during your holidays?

B: _____

_____

f) A: _____ Sunday morning?

B: _____

_____

g) A: _____ Friday evening?

B: _____

_____

h) A: _____ in two weeks?

B: _____

_____

i) A: _____ next Tuesday?

    B: _____

j) A: _____ next Wednesday?

    B: _____

        _____

3. In your own words, tell the class what each of these people should or shouldn't do in the following situations.

EXAMPLE: Ray is allergic to the sun.

He shouldn't sit in the sun.

OR

He should cover himself when he sits in the sun.

a) Sanira has very dry skin. She suffers from skin rashes.

b) Jamal isn't feeling well. He's coming down with a cold.

c) Carmen always hands in her assignments with a number of careless mistakes in them.

d) Raoul speaks English correctly but he has pronunciation problems.

e) My two-year-old son doesn't seem to hear me well when I talk to him.

f) My eight-year-old daughter is showing a lot of interest in music, especially piano.

g) Julio often criticizes and scolds his children in front of other people.

h) Luis' children spend most of their free time in front of the T.V.

i) Jasmina wants to study theatre arts. Her parents are against it. There is no future in it.

j) Little Dave thinks his cat is a toy. He plays with it too roughly. His parents don't say anything.

k) I just bought myself a knit suit and I noticed a run in the sleeve.

268

l)   This summer my teenage son will be bored if he stays home without anything to do.

4.   Rewrite each of the following requests more politely by using *Would you...*, *Will you...* and *Could you....*

Examples: Make the salad, please!

Would you please make the salad?

Will you please make the salad?

Could you please make the salad?

a)   Get me the paper, please!

b)   Take the dog for a walk, please!

c)   Leave the cat alone, please!

d)   Keep your dog on the leash, please!

e)   Water the plants, please!

f)   Empty the dishwasher, please!

g)   Take the garbage out, please!

h)   Spell your family name, please!

i)   Stop interrupting, please!

j)   Cut out that nonsense and get back to work, please!

k)   Stop fooling around and finish your work, please!

l)   Put away the puzzle, please!

m)   Make sure the door is locked, please!

n)   Remember to leave a note for the paper girl, please!

o)   Pick up a couple of steaks for dinner tonight, please!

5.   Work with a partner. Give your partner each of the instructions below. Your partner will make a request using the word *would*.

EXAMPLE: Offer someone a drink.

Would you like a drink?

a)   Ask someone to turn down the music.

b)   Ask someone to join you for dinner tonight.

c)   Ask your friend where he wants to go.

d)   Tell your friend you prefer to stay home tonight.

e)   Ask someone to sign her name in the register.

f)   Ask your friend if he wants to go dancing or catch a movie tonight.

g)   Tell a receptionist you want to speak to Mr. Roy.

h)   Tell someone to take a seat.

i)   Invite a friend to come to your party.

j)   Ask a writer to sign her autograph in your book.

k)   Invite a friend to play tennis with you tomorrow.

l)   Invite someone to test-ride your new bicycle.

m)   Ask someone to clean the carpets and polish the silver.

6.   Work with a partner. Give your partner each of the sentences below, beginning each with *I need someone to*.... Your partner will offer to do what you need, using *shall*.

Example: Make me something to eat.

I need someone to make me something to eat.

Shall I make you something to eat?

I need someone to:

a)   Set the table.

b)   Make me a cup of tea.

c)   Slice the potatoes.

d)   Add fresh mushrooms to the soup.

e)   Put some tabasco in the tomato sauce.

f)   Make me your special salad dressing.

g)   Pay the paper boy.

h)   Buy the theatre tickets.

i)   Get me something at the supermarket.

j)   Mail the letter for me.

k)   Pick me up at eight.

l)   Pick up my coat at the dry cleaners.

m) Translate the article for me.

n) Use some starch on my shirts.

o) Make me an extra set of keys.

7. Rewrite each of the following sentences using *would rather*. Be sure to keep the meaning the same.

EXAMPLE: I prefer to take time off in winter rather than in summer.

I'd rather take time off in winter than in summer.

a) Ron prefers to travel for a year before he goes to college.

b) Do you prefer to have a coffee or something cold to drink?

c) My parents prefer to pay cash rather than use a credit card.

d) I prefer to study by myself rather than with a classmate.

e) Are you buying yourself an evening dress?
   No, I prefer to buy a black suit.

f) Do you go out on your lunch break?
   No, I prefer to go to the gym or to the library.

g) Would you like to join us tonight?
   I prefer to stay home. I feel rather tired.

h) Let's buy some living room furniture.
   I prefer to spend the money on a trip.

i) Why don't you send the book back?
   I prefer to take it back myself.

j) Did you tell Susan about this?
   No, I prefer not to say anything.

k) Did she ask Chau to go over the document?
   No, she prefers to go over it herself.

l) My parents prefer to spend one week in the mountains rather than a month by the sea.
   Mine prefer to spend a month at the cottage.

8. Rewrite each of the following sentences using had better. Be sure to keep the meaning the same.

Example: I shouldn't drink any more wine!

I'd better not drink any more wine.

a) We don't have enough pop. We should buy some.

b) I suggest we get more traveller's cheques.

c) It's a good idea to bring the laundry in; it looks like rain.

d) I shouldn't drink coffee now or else I'll be up all night.

e) I should clean up the kitchen before Mom gets home or else she'll be angry at me.

f) We should confirm our flight or else we will lose our seats.

g) I suggest you type the assignment over if you don't want to lose marks for untidiness.

h) I think it's a good idea to install new double pane windows if we want to save energy.

i) I think it's better if you talk to Mrs. Morales if you want a transfer.

j) I advise you to see the doctor about this cold or else it will get worse.

k) Let's go home now or else we'll be stuck in the traffic.

l) I suggest you hurry if you don't want to miss your train.

9. Complete the following sentences with *must, mustn't* or any form of *have to*.

EXAMPLE: Stop arguing, Mike! You **must** follow Angela's instructions.

a) Here are 10 exercises. You _____ do them all but you _____ do at least five.

b) Rami! You _____ use that word again! Do you understand?

c) What _____ I _____ do to get a student loan?

d) Just a year ago, I _____ to start wearing glasses; now I'm wearing bifocals!

e) Did you call the plumber?

I _____ call the plumber! Sandra fixed the leak and changed the faucet.

f) The doctor says my brother _____ take potassium pills if he eats a banana every day.

g) You _____ play in that pond! It is polluted.

h) Canadians _____ pay a 7% tax on all goods and services.

i) The teacher says Mark _____ improve his marks if he wants to go to university.

j) My father says I _____ to buy a car. I can use his.

k) When I went to school in my country, all students _____ learn a second language. But this second language _____ be English.

l) The teacher says we _____ write the sentences. We can just fill in the blanks.

m) You can walk on the grass in the park but you _____ pick the flowers.

n) Why aren't you wearing your new dress?
When I took it out of the bag, I noticed a bad stain on the sleeve so I _____ take it back to the store.

o) We didn't expect you so early!
I _____ wait for the babysitter because my mother is home with the children.

p) I _____ have any orange juice anymore! The acidity gives me terrible stomachaches.

10. Work with a partner. Ask your partner each of the following questions. Your partner will complete the answers using *must* or *can't* to express deduction.

EXAMPLE: Where is Jamila?

She **must be** in her room. I can hear her typewriter.

a) Does Rosa know Effat?
She _____ him. They both belong to the same tennis club.

b) How does she pay for the stamps?

She _____ petty cash. She pays for everything under $15.

c) Does Denise understand Italian?

She _____ Italian. She spent a year in Italy.

d) Does Samir clean the stairs of the building?

He _____ them. No one else does.

e) Do they use their dry leaves for compost?

They _____ for compost. They have a large composter in their backyard.

f) Does he supervise the workers?

He _____ them. He knows nothing about construction.

g) Is this sweater wool?

It _____ . It feels like nylon.

h) Is this woman new here?

She _____ . She can't remember her boss's name!

i) Does Renée hold an important position in the company?

She _____ . A secretary takes all her incoming calls.

j) I think Aziza and Ahmed are already back in Pakistan!

They _____ . I saw them at the mall this morning.

k) Is this paint water- or oil-based?

It _____ water-based! It washed off in clear water.

l) Do you think Helen is German?

She _____ German. She doesn't speak a word of German. Besides, she has a thick Slavic accent.

m) These are the keys to the garage!

They _____ . They're too small for the lock.

n) What time is your flight?

At two o'clock, but we _____ at the airport two hours before departure time.

11. Work with a partner. Ask your partner each of the following questions. Your partner will answer in complete sentences using *may* or *might,* and adding an expression such as *I'm not sure, I don't know* or *I have no idea.*

EXAMPLE: Is the counsellor available five days a week?

He may be available five days a week, I'm not sure.

a) Is the elevator working?

b) Does Roger know about the emergency meeting?

c) Will Danuta make us some chicken soup?

d) Will Rosa make the curtains for the staff room?

e) Is Juanita hiring new staff?

f) Is Andy in charge of the stockroom now?

g) Is Marco consulting a lawyer?

h) Is Francesca training new staff?

i) Will Renata have to wear a uniform?

j) Will your mother get the job?

k) Does José want to go back to Portugal?

l) Will Rita and Carlos have a big wedding?

m) Will Tamara's parents retire in Florida?

n) Will Carmella take up hairdressing?

o) Is Balbir feeling better with the new medication?

p) Is Joanna applying for the new position in sales?

12. Complete the following sentences with the correct form of the appropriate modal.

EXAMPLES: **Will** you please follow me?

If it's still raining this afternoon, I **might** not go out.

a) _____ I borrow your calculator?

Of course. Go ahead.

b) No, you _____ take over the job right away! You _____ go

through a training session first.

c) He's tall and blond and his name is Finnish. He _____ be Finnish, he _____ be Danish.

d) Stevie, I'm telling you again! You _____ tell lies.

e) _____ I leave now?
If you've finished your assignment, you _____ .

f) The Keep Out sign means you _____ enter.

g) She has a terrible back problem. She _____ wear such uncomfortable shoes.

h) If you want to drive to the East Coast on your holidays, and you don't have a car, you _____ rent one.

i) Sorry, Clara! You _____ play outside yet. You _____ eat your lunch first.

j) This dictionary is just excellent! You _____ get yourself one.

k) I'm sorry I'm late! I _____ wait for the bus for over 20 minutes.

l) If you want to be an electrician, you _____ have a license.

m) Sara failed her bar exam!
Poor Sara! She _____ be very upset.

n) I need an English/Amharic dictionary right away. Do you know who's got one?
Why don't you go to the school library. They _____ have one there.

o) When the property taxes and the mortgage rates went up, my friends _____ keep their house any longer. They _____ sell it.

p) Danielle's cough is getting worse! We _____ call the doctor.

q) My doctor says I _____ cut down on sweets, but I _____ never resist ice cream and cream pies.

r) _____ I borrow a cup of sugar? I _____ go to the store right now.

s) I have to lay off 10 people because of the slowdown in the company.

That's terrible! You _____ be under terrible stress.

t) _____ you please repeat that last sentence for me? I didn't get it.

u) Did you finally buy yourself a new coat?

I did, but the sleeves are too long. I _____ shorten them.

v) The teachers took the students to the zoo. The students _____ pay $5.00 to get in but the teachers _____ pay at all.

13. Rewrite the following sentences using a modal that expresses each of the ideas listed below.

EXAMPLE: Terry takes a course in blueprint reading. It is required.

Terry must take a course in blueprint reading.

a) Terry takes a course in blueprint reading.

i) I'm giving him this advice.

ii) It's probable.

iii) It's not necessary.

b) Rosa attends the meeting.

i) It's necessary.

ii) It's advisable.

iii) It's not possible.

iv) It's not required.

c) They finish work by 5:00.

i) It's expected.

ii) They're not capable.

iii) It's possible they won't.

iv) It's not necessary.

d) We take reference books out of the library.

i) It's not allowed.

ii) It's prohibited.

iii) Is it possible? (question)

e) I eat shellfish.

i) With my allergies, it's not a good idea.

ii) It's not possible. I react to it.

iii) My doctor ordered me not to.

iv) It's all right. I'm allowed to.

f) You drive my car.

  i) You have a license and you're careful enough.

  ii) I don't allow you to! You don't have a license.

  iii) I advise you to.

  iv) It's not advisable if you're nervous.

g) The manager is in her office.

  i) I expect her to be there.

  ii) I'm sure she is there.

  iii) It's not possible. I left her in the cafeteria a few minutes ago.

  iv) It's possible, but I have no idea.

h) Zoran has a tool box.

  i) I'm sure he does.

  ii) It's necessary! He's a mechanic.

  iii) He had no choice.

  iv) It's possible but I'm not sure.

EXPRESS YOURSELF

1. Work with a partner. Ask your partner each of the following questions. Your partner will answer in complete sentences using *may* or *might*, and adding an expression such as *I'm not sure, I don't know* or *I have no idea*.

EXAMPLE: Will you be studying for your math test tonight?

I may study tonight. I am not sure.

a) What are you doing tonight?

b) What are you having for dinner tonight?

c) Are you visiting a friend soon, and when?

d)   Are you watching T.V. tonight? If yes, what program?

e)   What are you doing this weekend?

f)   Are you taking any holidays this year?

g)   How will you spend your next long weekend?

h)   Are you going shopping soon? What are you buying yourself?

i)   Are you going to take another English course?

j)   What are your plans for the future?

k)   What do you think the weather will be like tomorrow?

l)   Do you think vegetables and fruits will be cheaper this summer?

m)   Will income tax go up or down?

n)   Will the tax on goods and services go up or down?

o)   Will prices of houses go up or down?

2.   Work with a partner. Ask your partner the following questions. Your partner will answer in complete sentences using a modal each time.

a)   What should you do if you see a fire?

b)   What must you do if there is a fire in your building?

c)   What may happen to me if I speed on the highway?

d)   What can people do if they need to buy furniture but don't have the money to?

e)   How can people pay for purchases?

f)   What do you have to do around the house?

g)   What language do you have to know in order to get a job in this country?

h)   What qualifications do you need before you can work in your profession?

i)   What should I do if I want to change careers?

j)   What mustn't people do while pumping gas?

k)   What couldn't you do as a teenager?

l)   What does this sign, No Diving in Swimming Pool, mean?

m) What does this advertisement, Delivery people with own car needed, mean?

n) Why is it important for an electrician to have a license?

o) What can people do with a credit card?

p) I am writing a paper on Child Welfare and I need statistics and a lot of information. Where can I get them?

q) I am an auto mechanic from Europe. What should I do if I want to work in my profession and why?

r) What will you be doing at this time tomorrow?

s) What will you be doing at this time next week?

3. Work with a partner. Tell your partner, then write about the following:

a) Three things you can do now but couldn't do some time ago.

b) Three things you can't do now but could do some time ago.

c) Three things you should do but neglect to do.

d) Three things you shouldn't do but do anyway.

e) Three things you don't have to do now because you're an adult.

f) Three things you didn't have to do as a child.

4. Imagine and tell a partner what you will be doing a year from now.

5. Talk to a partner about your plans. Tell your partner what you may do, and then write your plans down.

6. Think about an imaginary wealthy person. Make assumptions, three with *must* and three with *can't*. Tell a partner about your assumptions and then write them down.

7. Think about an elderly person. Make assumptions with *must* and *can't*. Tell a partner about your assumptions and then write them down.

8. Tell a partner a few things one must do or "should" do before travelling abroad. Then write about them.

9. Explain to a partner what one should do before applying for a job. Then write your ideas down.

10. Work in pairs. The following are introductions to short dialogues or conversations. With a partner, make up a short conversation. In each response, you must include a modal.

EXAMPLE:
A: What are you doing tonight?

B: I'm not going out. I have to study for my exam on Monday.

A: Why don't you take a break and come to the movies with us? You can study on the weekend.

B: I suppose I could but I'd rather start getting ready for my exam tonight.

a) Let's go swimming.

b) Are you looking for a job in a bank?

c) Do you speak French?

d) What about apple pie and ice cream?

Appendix I

IRREGULAR VERBS IN THE SIMPLE PAST TENSE AND THE PAST PARTICIPLE AND PRONUNCIATION

The following list gives the three main parts of 140 common irregular verbs: the infinitive, the simple past tense and past participle. Irregular verbs fall into three groups:

Group 1:   All three parts are pronounced identically.
Group 2:   Two parts are pronounced identically.
Group 3:   No parts are pronounced identically.

GROUP 1

Infinitive	Simple Past	Past Participle
bet /bɛt/	bet /bɛt/	bet /bɛt/
beat /bit/	beat /bit/	beat /bit/
bid /bɪd/	bid /bɪd/	bid /bɪd/
burst /bɜst/	burst /bɜst/	burst /bɜst/
cast /kæst/	cast /kæst/	cast /kæst/
cost /kɔst/	cost /kɔst/	cost /kɔst/
cut /kʌt/	cut /kʌt/	cut /kʌt/
hit /hɪt/	hit /hɪt/	hit /hɪt/
hurt /hɜt/	hurt /hɜt/	hurt /hɜt/
let /lɛt/	let /lɛt/	let /lɛt/
put /pʊt/	put /pʊt/	put /pʊt/
quit /kwɪt/	quit /kwɪt/	quit /kwɪt/
		(*also*: "quitted" /kwɪtɪd/)
set /sɛt/	set /sɛt/	set /sɛt/
shut /ʃʌt/	shut /ʃʌt/	shut /ʃʌt/
split /splɪt/	split /splɪt/	split /splɪt/
spread /sprɛd/	spread /sprɛd/	spread /sprɛd/
wed /wɛd/	wed /wɛd/	wed /wɛd/
		(*also*: "wedded" /wɛdɪd/)

GROUP 2

Infinitive	Simple Past	Past Participle
become /bɪkʌm/	became /bɪkeɪm/	become /bɪkʌm/

Infinitive	Simple Past	Past Participle
bend /bɛnd/	bent /bɛnt/	bent /bɛnt/
bind /baɪnd/	bound /baʊnd/	bound /baʊnd/
bleed /blid/	bled /blɛd/	bled /blɛd/
breed /brid/	bred /brɛd/	bred /brɛd/
bring /brɪŋ/	brought /brɔt/	brought /brɔt/
build /bɪld/	built /bɪlt/	built /bɪlt/
burn /bɜn/	burnt /bɜnt/	burnt /bɜnt/
buy /baɪ/	bought /bɔt/	bought /bɔt/
catch /kætʃ/	caught /kɔt/	caught /kɔt/
cling /klɪŋ/	clung /klʌŋ/	clung /klʌŋ/
come /kʌm/	came /keɪm/	come /kʌm/
creep /krip/	crept /krɛpt/	crept /krɛpt/
deal /dil/	dealt /dɛlt/	dealt /dɛlt/
dig /dɪg/	dug /dʌg/	dug /dʌg/
dream /drim/	dreamt /drɛmt/	dreamt /drɛmt/
feed /fid/	fed /fɛd/	fed /fɛd/
feel /fil/	felt /fɛlt/	felt /fɛlt/

GROUP 2

Infinitive	**Simple Past**	**Past Participle**
fight /faɪt/	fought /fɔt/	fought /fɔt/
find /faɪnd/	found /faʊnd/	found /faʊnd/
flee /fli/	fled /flɛd/	fled /flɛd/
get /gɛt/	got /gɔt/	got /gɔt/
grind /graɪnd/	ground /graʊnd/	ground /graʊnd/
hang /hæŋ/	hung /hʌŋ/	hung /hʌŋ/
hear /hir/	heard /hɜd/	heard /hɜd/
hold /hold/	held /hɛld/	held /hɛld/
lay /leɪ/	laid /leɪd/	laid /leɪd/
lead /lid/	led /lɛd/	led /lɛd/
lean /lin/	leant /lɛnt/	leant /lɛnt/
leap /lip/	leapt /lɛpt/	leapt /lɛpt/
learn /lɜn/	learnt /lɜnt/ (*also:* "learned" /lɜnd/)	learnt /lɜnt learned /lɜnd/)
lend /lɛnd/	lent /lɛnt/	lent /lɛnt/
light /laɪt/	lit /lɪt/	lit /lɪt/
lose /luz/	lost /lɔst/	lost /lɔst/

make /meɪk/	made /meɪd/	made /meɪd/
mean /min/	meant /mɛnt/	meant /mɛnt/
meet /mit/	met /mɛt/	met /mɛt/
pay /peɪ/	paid /peɪd/	paid /peɪd/
read /rid/	read /rɛd/	read /rɛd/
run /rʌn/	ran /ræn/	run /rʌn/
say /seɪ/	said /sɛd/	said /sɛd/
sell /sɛl/	sold /sold/	sold /sold/
send /sɛnd/	sent /sɛnt/	sent /sɛnt/
shine /ʃaɪn/	shone /ʃon/	shone /ʃon/
shoot /ʃut/	shot /ʃɔt/	shot /ʃɔt/
sit /sɪt/	sat /sæt/	sat /sæt/
sleep /slip/	slept /spɛlt/	slept /slɛpt/
sling /slɪŋ/	slung /slʌŋ/	slung /slʌŋ/
spell /spɛl/	spelt /spɛlt/	spelt /spɛlt/
	(*also*: "spelled" /spɛld/	spelled /spɛld/)
spend /spɛnd/	spent /spɛnt/	spent /spɛnt/
spill /spɪl/	spilt /spɪlt/	spilt /spɪlt/
	(*also*: "spilled" /spɪld/	spilled /spɪld/)
spin /spɪn/	spun /spʌn/	spun /spʌn/
spit /spɪt/	spat /spæt/	spat /spæt/
	(*also*: "spit" /spɪt/	spit /spɪt/)
spoil /spɔil/	spoilt /spɔɪlt/	spoilt /spɔɪlt/
	(*also*: "spoiled /spɔɪld/	spoiled /spɔɪld/)
stand /stænd/	stood /stʊd/	stood /stʊd/
stick /stɪk/	stuck /stʌk/	stuck /stʌk/
sting /stɪŋ/	stung /stʌŋ/	stung /stʌŋ/
strike /straɪk/	struck /strʌk/	struck /strʌk/
string /strɪŋ/	strung /strʌŋ/	strung /strʌŋ/
sweep /swip/	swept /swɛpt/	swept /swɛpt/
swing /swɪŋ/	swung /swʌŋ/	swung /swʌŋ/
teach /titʃ/	taught /tɔt/	taught /tɔt/

GROUP 2

Infinitive	Simple Past	Past Participle
tell /tɛl/	told /told/	told /told/
think /θɪŋk/	thought /θɔt/	thought /θɔt/

weep /wip/	wept /wɛpt/	wept /wɛpt/
win /wɪn/	won /wɔn/	won /wɔn/
wind /waɪnd/	wound /waʊnd/	wound /waʊnd/
wring /rɪŋ/	wrung /rʌŋ/	wrung /rʌŋ/

GROUP 3

bear /bɛr/	bore /bɔr/	born /bɔrn/
begin /bɪgɪn/	began /bɪgæn/	begun /bɪgʌn/
bite /baɪt/	bit /bɪt/	bitten /bɪtɪn/
blow /blo/	blew /blu/	blown /blon/
break /breɪk/	broke /brok/	broken /brokɪn/
choose /tʃuz/	chose /tʃoz/	chosen /tʃozɪn/
dive /daɪv/	drew /dru/	drawn /drɔn/
do /du/	did /dɪd/	done /dʌn/
draw /drɔ/	drew /dru/	drawn /drɔn/
drink /drɪŋk/	drank /dræŋk/	drunk /drʌŋk/
drive /draɪv/	drove /drov/	driven /drɪvɪn/
eat /it/	ate /eɪt/	eaten /itɪn/
fall /fɔl/	fell /fɛl/	fallen /fɔlɪn/
fly /flaɪ/	flew /flu/	flown /flon/
forsake /fɔrseɪk/	forsook /fɔrs k/	forsaken /fɔrseɪkɪn/
freeze /friz/	froze /froz/	frozen /frozɪn/
forget /fɔrgɛt/	forgot /fɔrgɔt/	forgotten /fɔrgvtɪn/
give /gɪv/	gave /geɪv/	given /gɪvɪn/
go /go/	went /wɛnt/	gone /gɔn/
grow /gro/	grew /gru/	grown /gron/
hew /hyu/	hewed /hyud/	hewn /hyun/
hide /haɪd/	hid /hɪd/	hidden /hɪdɪn/
know /no/	knew /nju/	known /non/
lie /laɪ/	lay /leɪ/	laid /leɪd/
mow /mo/	mowed /mod/	mown /mon/
		(*also:* "mowed" /mod/)
ride /raɪd/	rode /rod/	ridden /rɪdɪn/
ring /rɪŋ/	rang /ræŋ/	rung /rʌŋ/
rise /raɪz/	rose /roz/	risen /rɪzɪn/
saw /sɔ/	sawed /sɔd/	sawn /sɔn/
		(*also:* "sawed" /sɔd/
see /si/	saw /sɔ/	seen /sin/

sew /so/	sewed /sod/	sewn /son/ (*also:* "sewed" /sod/)
shake /ʃeɪk/	shook /ʃʊk/	shaken /ʃeɪkɪn/
shrink /ʃrɪŋk/	shrank /ʃræŋk/	shrunk /ʃrʌŋk/
show /ʃo/	showed /ʃod/	shown /ʃon/
sink /sɪŋk/	sank /sæk/	sunk /sʌŋk/
sing /sɪŋ/	sang /sæŋ/	sung /sʌŋ/
slay /sleɪ/	slew /slu/	slain /sleɪn/
smell /smɛl/	smelled /smɛld/	smelt /smɛlt/ (*also:* "smelled" /smɛld/)

GROUP 3

Infinitive	**Simple Past**	**Past Participle**
sow /so/	sowed /sod/	sown /son/ (*also:* "sowed" /sod/)
speak /spik/	spoke /spok/	spoken /sokɪn/
spring /sprɪŋ/	sprang /spræŋ/	sprung /sprʌŋ/
steal /stil/	stole /stol/	stolen /stolɪn/
stink /stɪŋk/	stank /stæŋk/	stunk /stʌŋk/
stride /straɪd/	strode /strod/	stridden /strɪdɪn/
swear /swɛr/	swore /swɔr/	sworn /swɔrn/
swell /swɛl/	swelled /swɛld/	swollen /swɔlɪn/ (*also:* "swelled" /swɛld/)
swim /swɪm/	swam /swæm/	swum /swʌm/
take /teɪk/	took /tʊk/	taken /teɪkɪn/
tear /tɛr/	tore /tɔr/	torn /tɔrn/
throw /θro/	threw /θru/	thrown /θron/
wake /weɪk/	woke /wok/	woken /wokɪn/
wear /wɛr/	wore /wɔr/	worn /wɔrn/
weave /wiv/	wove /wov/	woven /wovɪn/
write /wraɪt/	wrote /wrot/	written /wrɪtɪn/

Index   *[Entries without page numbers refer to Volume B]*